Memoirs
While Memory Lasts

by Richard Hoskin

For Jimi —
Enjoy!

Richard Hoskin

The Cornish Chronicle
Publisher
Cold Spring, Kentucky

The Cornish Chronicle

Publisher
Cold Spring, Kentucky

Copyright © by Richard John Collins Hoskin
All rights reserved

ISBN 13: 978-0-9863339-1-0

Dedication

This book is dedicated to my family in Cornwall and America, including my forebears who filled my veins with Celtic blood, and my fingers with the itch to write their stories down; to my children and my grandchildren to whom I pass on my heritage and on whom I count to read every word. Grateful thanks to my wife Penny for designing the book cover and interior and her tireless help in improving my writing. Thanks also to the Monday Morning Writers Group whose encouragement and constructive criticism over the years contributed greatly, especially to Maureen ("Mo") Conlan and Mary Anne Sanders for their conscientious editorial insights and sharpness of eyes for accuracy.

P.S. Note to grandchildren. If you read every word of these memoirs you may find clues to the hiding place for my will, from which you may benefit – Granfer

Book interior and cover design by Cynthia Osborne Hoskin
Photo credits: John L. Rapson, Liskeard; Wikipedia

This book is available for special promotions and premiums.
Address requests to cornishchronicle@gmail.com

Table of Contents

Our Gang and Other Warfare 1
Kizzling Doney 19
The Best Cat in the World 23
Constitution of an Ox 31
Boatbuilders 39
Fag! 45
Breakthrough 55
Brilliant Minds 61
Eccentrics 69
Top of the World 75
Ancestry 81
Gustatory Defeat 85
Special Relationship 89
Gentlemen's Game 93
LUGOT 103
Wonderful Women 109
I Went Back 119
Passwords 123
Teamwork 135
Merrie Olde 139
Jailbird 145
Spring Cleaning 151
Wimbledon 153
Star 157
Piece of Cake 161
Nearing Journey's End 171
Eulogy 177

Our Gang and Other Warfare

When I was a little boy in England I heard my parents talking about the crisis. They talked about it day after day. I didn't know what a crisis was, and they didn't explain it to me. I looked for it out of the dining room window. I imagined it to be some kind of a dark cloud, but the sky was clear. It was a perfect early autumn day.

I was usually out playing in my red pedal car while my parents listened to the six o'clock evening news on the BBC wireless. But that evening when I came in towards the end of the news bulletin, I couldn't help noticing that their faces looked grave. They told my big sisters and me that Germany had invaded Poland. It was September 1, 1939. I was six years old.

They explained that this meant that war would almost certainly break out, and we would have to be brave. Everybody had hoped there would be peace forever. I had heard a BBC broadcast when the Prime Minister, Neville Chamberlain, came back from meeting Herr Hitler in Munich. He promised us "peace in our time". He said in that rather quavery voice of his:

"I have in my hand a piece of paper. . . "

Three days later on September 3rd Britain kept its promise to come to the aid of Poland and declared war on Nazi Germany. So much for a piece of paper.

We lived in a remote agricultural area of Cornwall in a small town called Liskeard on the southwestern tip of the British Isles. It didn't seem remote to me because I lived there. My father said there wasn't much worth bombing, just a few pigs and cows and sheep. That made me feel better, but I wasn't taking any chances.

I brought my red pedal car into the conservatory at the back of the house to shield it from the "crisis", which by then I understood to be war and bombs. The conservatory probably didn't provide much protection, because it was made of glass, but at least a passing

Messerschmitt fighter wouldn't see my car. My red car had been the fastest of all the children's wheeled toys in our neighborhood until Jean Shearsmith got a chain driven tricycle for her birthday. It had big wheels and she could go really fast, but I still didn't want my red car to be bombed.

I did go a bit off Jean when she got her big tricycle, but we were still good playmates in games that girls could join in. I had actually married Jean Shearsmith when we were both five, because she was pretty nice. She wore a lace curtain from their dining room for the wedding, and I wore the paper collar that came from the laundry where her father had his shirts and collars starched. My big sister Pat took official photographs with her Brownie camera.

Soon there was another reason I kept my red pedal car hidden. The government announced that it was going to commandeer civilian lorries for the war effort. The army needed more transportation for essential materials. They even came and collected the fleet of red lorries that delivered Corona to our house, painted them khaki and used them to carry war materials. Corona was a delicious fizzy pop that came in different colors in special bottles, the reusable kind with a ceramic stopper with a rubber washer held on tightly by a sort of wire cage that snapped it shut. There were four bottles in a wooden box with dividers. The driver would pick up our box with its empty bottles and deliver a new supply every week. No more Corona until the war was over. It was not essential and everyone had to do one's bit.

Lots of things had to go towards the war effort. The government asked people to turn in their old aluminium pots and pans to be melted down and used to build aeroplanes. They sent men to cut down the beautiful ornamental railings protecting the older houses and important buildings. One old spinster lady who lived in Manley Terrace complained that she had just had her railings freshly painted. "That's all right, ma'am," said one of the men, "we'll take 'em, paint and all." Seemed an awful pity. They were made of heavy cast iron, not much use for building aeroplanes.

A new boy came to live nearby about that time. His name was Leslie Solt and he was an evacuee. He had been evacuated to the country from his home in a big city that was too dangerous with the air raids. His father had been called up into the army and his mother had sent him to live with his grandparents in Cornwall where he would be safer. His grandfather was the foreman of the sawmill down beyond the Great Western Railway station. It used to get all the timber from the Duchy Woods. The bigger trees were sawn into planks for building, and the smaller pine trees were made into pit props and sent to the coalmines in Wales.

The sawmill used coal for the steam engines that drove their circular saws so they were also in the business of selling coal. They delivered sacks of coal to their customers in the town on a flat wagon drawn by an old carthorse called Paddy. We had a coal cellar under our house where they emptied the hundredweight sacks onto a pile. Sometimes I got to ride on the wagon on the way home from school, but I didn't help unload the sacks of coal because you had to be really strong.

Leslie had a collection of toy soldiers and army trucks and tanks and artillery. He had a subscription to a magazine with articles about warfare and pictures of soldiers, weapons, navy ships, and air force planes. He was really interested in that kind of thing.

Leslie had a good idea. The sawmill produced a huge pile of sawdust, so he thought we could dig out the middle of it and build a fort that would make us safe from an air raid or even an invasion. If there was an invasion, the German soldiers might not notice us. In case they did we could make wooden rifles that they might think were real, and they would keep their distance. We could also go to the toy shop in the town and use our pocket money to buy tin helmets that would make us look like real soldiers.

We built a really good fort with a main front trench, connecting side trenches, and a foxhole, just like the plans we saw in Leslie's magazine. We spent most of the time playing in the sawdust pile with the toy army trucks and artillery guns shooting match sticks at imaginary enemies. There was a heavy thunderstorm a couple of weeks later, and when we went back, our fort had been washed away.

Then we worried about what we would do if an invasion came. The government stopped the ringing of all church bells summoning people to church on Sundays and even for practicing the complicated peals, because the bells all over the country would be used solely as a signal to warn people if an invasion did come. There were rumors that the German paratroopers would be disguised as nuns to deceive us. Leslie and I thought that seemed awfully unsporting. Anyway, wouldn't it be a bit cumbersome to jump out of a plane with a parachute and wearing a nun's habit?

Bad dreams haunted me after I borrowed one of Leslie's magazines to read in bed at night. There was a picture of a German paratrooper wearing a gas mask and armed with a sub-machine gun, ammunition belts, and hand grenades. He looked fearsome, and I dreamt that he climbed into my bedroom one night. After that I was allowed to sleep in a camp bed in my parents' bedroom for several weeks.

Early on in the war we civilians were all issued with gas masks. The government was afraid that the Germans would use poison gas again, as they had in World War I in the trenches in France. The gas masks were made of black rubber with straps to hold them to one's head and had a flexible transparent panel on the front to see through. They were packed in a cubic cardboard box about a foot square that had to be carried at all times. My mother made a cloth bag to hold mine with a strap I could sling across my shoulder. It was pretty neat, and some of the other children's mothers copied the idea.

At school the teachers helped us practice putting our gas masks on. We kept the boxes under our desks. We had to take out the mask, unfold it, stick our chins in and pull the mask up over our faces. Then we had to breathe in through a circular filter about three inches in diameter that was in front of our noses and mouths. When we breathed out, our breath blew out through the sides next to our cheeks. At first your breath would cloud over the transparent panel and you could not see. I tried not to be afraid. One of the girls did get scared and grabbed her mask by the front and pulled it up over her chin and off her face. She was so relieved, but the teacher made her try again until she got used to it. The girl cried, but the teacher was trying to be kind.

Soon we were issued identity cards. The government was afraid of spies being dropped by parachute in the middle of the night or landed by submarine and rubber raft in one of the coves on the coast of Cornwall. They could pass themselves off as English and transmit secrets to the Germans, such as where the concrete pill-boxes and the land mines were placed to defend against the invasion. If a policeman or a sentry stopped you by mistake, showing your identity card would prove you were British.

My sister Pam made an identity card for Jimmy Monk, my favorite soft toy. She suggested that name because he was a monkey. The card used his full name, James, and with its official looking seals it looked almost like a real one. Pam was knitting warm woolen gloves for soldiers at the time and gave me khaki wool and knitting needles to make a scarf. She cast on enough stitches to make it eight inches wide and taught me plain knitting, thinking purl might be a bit complicated. I planned to make it about four or five feet long so it would be warm for the winter. Unfortunately, I got busy doing other things, so when it got to two inches long my sister cast off the stitches, and we made a scarf for Jimmy Monk instead.

I loved Jimmy Monk and kept him a long time. He was born in a London toy shop. He had a monkey's face and was dressed as a pageboy with a pink uniform and a black cap. My mother gave him to me for my fourth birthday before the war when we were on our way back from Denmark. I had stayed in Copenhagen with her for three months where she had to go to have special treatment. The Danish doctors were kind, but said she had Lupus, and they had to burn infection off her face and nose. She had been beautiful but she wore hats with veils after that.

The Danish people were friendly and welcoming. I felt sorry for them when the Germans invaded and occupied their country, the same fate suffered by most countries in Europe. They were brave and resisted in little ways all through the war.

We felt safer at home when the Local Defence Volunteers were formed. With no real weapons or uniforms at first, they wore armlets with "L.D.V." on them and drilled with pitchforks and scythes. They might have slowed down invaders for a while, but they probably couldn't have stopped them. Eventually they got uniforms, real rifles and Bren guns, and their name was changed to the Home Guard. Uncle Dick was persuaded to join, because he had been in a machine gun unit in the Great War.

My father was also in the Great War, stationed in India, Mesopotamia, Palestine, and Egypt. He brought back an artillery shell that was used to hold our front door open. He was very patriotic and thought Hitler should be given a big punch on the jaw, so I think he wanted to join up again, but he was too old. Instead he volunteered for Air Raid Precautions. The uniform was tough navy blue trousers with a matching blouse kind of jacket with an armlet with "A.R.P." on it and a white tin hat saying "Senior Warden". His tin helmet did not come from the toy shop.

Soon there was a post at the end of our front garden with a sloping board painted greenish yellow that would detect mustard gas by changing color. Then we were issued with a stirrup pump to put out fires caused by incendiary bombs. One afternoon the wardens had to attend a demonstration to learn how to use the stirrup pumps. A fire was started in a field, and the instructor demonstrated how to crawl towards it on your belly and put it out. None of the wardens wanted to crawl on their bellies, partly because they didn't want to get their clothes muddy, and partly because they were all old and portly. They let me take a turn, and I plopped right down on my tummy and sprayed water enthusiastically all over the fire. After that Tom Lang (who was the owner of the sawmill where Leslie Solt's grandfather worked) painted "Junior Warden" on my tin helmet to make me official.

Even though Liskeard was just a small town surrounded by farms, we were actually a mere twenty miles from the city of Plymouth and its neighbor Devonport, which was a Royal Navy base and dockyard. Liskeard's newly installed streetlights were turned off. The idea was to prevent us from being attacked and to confuse the navigators in German bombers looking for landmarks at night. The air raid wardens made sure that every house blacked out all windows and outside doors. My mother bought blackout fabric and criss-crossed adhesive tape on the windows to prevent splintered glass from flying inward should there be a bomb blast.

Soon the air raids started, the Blitz, night after night after night. We could see the searchlights raking the sky beyond the ridge behind our house, sometimes lighting up the barrage balloons, and we could hear the antiaircraft guns firing and then the bombs going off. Soon the sky was filled with smoke, lit up orange and red with the fires from incendiary bombs.

Barrage balloons were like great big fat sausages made of fabric, attached by cables to the ground. They were filled with hydrogen to make them float up, and were supposed to get in the way of bombers trying to fly low over their targets.

During the day Gloster Gladiator fighters patrolled the skies. They were biplanes, slow and not much good at night, with a top speed of 250 mph. They were armed with four .303" machine guns. I have often thought how brave the Royal Air Force pilots must have been to try and defend us with equipment that was outclassed. The enemy German Messerschmidt fighters were fast monoplanes with speeds as high as 350 mph, armed with 7.92 mm machine guns and 20 mm cannons.

The new Hurricanes and Spitfires joined the fight, just in time for the Battle of Britain. They were in the sky most of that summer, and we often saw the white contrails as they patrolled the area around Devonport. My sister gave me a kit for making a model Spitfire out of balsa wood, complete with R.A.F. roundels and paint. I rather messed up the camouflage paint on the top, but the duck egg blue on the underside was quite neat. We wished we could have seen some dogfights, but the R.A.F. fighters had chased the German Junkers bombers and Messerschmidt fighters too far away from where we lived.

The town council dug a pit by the hedge of the field behind our house and roofed it with telegraph poles to make an air raid shelter. But my father said that as Senior Warden we should set a personal example. My Uncle Dick was a builder and he had his men dig a pit and build a concrete air raid shelter to a government design in the part of the back garden where my father usually planted cabbages.

My father was "Digging for Victory" and keeping us fed with peas, beans, carrots, turnips and potatoes throughout the war. He also planted apple and pear trees. My mother was grateful for any food, because it was hard for her to stretch the rations to feed her family. In a way, I think she took pride in making do.

Most things were rationed, including meat, butter, margarine and lard, jam, tea, sugar, and sweets. We each got one egg a week and three pints of milk. Fresh fruit and vegetables were generally not rationed but were often in short supply. We did not need ration books for offal, and the butcher liked my mother so our meat included a lot of liver and kidneys, hearts and sweetbreads, all delicious. My parents refused to supplement our supplies by buying on the black market because it would be setting a bad example.

All of Cornwall was near the sea, and fish were not rationed. Younger fishermen had gone off to fight in the Royal Navy or into the Merchant Marine to dodge the U-Boats and help bring in most of Britain's food from overseas, including weird but welcome concoctions from America like Spam and dried eggs. However, the older fishermen managed to keep going with a smaller fleet at home. Mr. Minards would bring up fish from Looe on the train in an old baby carriage every Monday on market day. Friends kept chickens, so we got fresh eggs and the occasional stewing fowl. At least the sparse food, grey bread and absence of sweets meant there were few overweight people around.

Meanwhile, the effects of the war were being felt more "up country" (as we Cornish people said) in the industrial cities like Birmingham and Coventry and London, rather than close to home around Plymouth and Devonport.

There was excitement when fishing boats and other small boats sailed across the English Channel to a small place called Dunkirk on the coast of France to rescue the remains of the British Expeditionary Force. To hear some people talk it sounded like a victory, but a lot of the grown ups were looking worried, and the men who came back from Dunkirk looked tired and not very cheerful.

The new Prime Minister, Winston Churchill, growled at us over the wireless and told us we had to fight the enemy everywhere until we won.

We shall never surrender, he said. All the gallant countries in the British Empire would come to our aid. We shall fight on the landing grounds, we shall fight on the beaches. Well, there weren't any landing grounds near us, and the beaches were covered with barbed wire and mines, so they would be dangerous. But we would manage to do our bit.

Then Mr. Churchill told us that *HMS Prince of Wales* and *HMS Repulse* had been sunk by the Japanese off Malaya. I knew where

Malaya was because of my stamp collection. All the stamps from countries in the Empire had the king's head on them. And I knew about the battleships because I had got *The Wonder Book of the Royal Navy* for Christmas. Those two were big ships with big crews, an awful loss.

Even though there was a lot of bad war news, there were some things to be joyful about. One of them was right in our town. In 1940 we celebrated the seven hundredth anniversary of Liskeard being created a royal borough with its own mayor and aldermen and corporation. Richard, Earl of Cornwall, brother of Henry III, granted Liskeard a Charter in 1240. Liskeard was important in those days because it was a "stannary" town, which meant that it regulated the tin industry and could collect fees and taxes. In 1294, and for a long time afterwards, Liskeard returned two Members to Parliament.

Anyway, our air raid shelter in the back garden was finally built. It had a front entrance sheltered by a concrete wall and an escape hatch with sandbags at the back. Inside there were bunks made of wooden frames with chicken wire tacked to them where we could sleep at night and shelves to store tinned food and bottles of water. From then on we would get up in the middle of the night when the terrifying air raid siren wailed and howled. Trooping down to the shelter in our dressing gowns, we tried to sleep through the noise of the raid.

One night as we were walking through the kitchen in the dark, a frightful fluorescent light caught my eye. It looked like a ghost. I jumped back. Gaining courage, as it didn't move, I went to investigate. It turned out to be the glow from the eyes of the fish heads on the counter, set there until I could cook them for my cat Tigger. We would look forward to the siren sounding the "All Clear" so that we could safely return to our own beds.

The war brought a lot of new children to our town. John Wilkins and his cousin Jennifer came from Plymouth to stay with their aunt and uncle who were neighbors. Jennifer was a bit young, but John was fun to play with. There were also Robin and Brian whose mothers were sisters. They rented a nearby house with each family living on one floor. They didn't need that much space because their fathers were in the R.A.F. and were away a lot of the time, although they sometimes came home on leave.

There was also a family called Crump who rented the upper floor next door. Captain Crump was in the army. They had a small son named Robert. One day he leaned out of the window too far and fell on to the gravel path below. Fortunately he was unharmed, perhaps because he was well fed despite the rationing. My sisters went around saying, "Bump, bump, went plump Robert Crump!" They usually had a helpful comment on what went on around us.

We often had people billeted with us, especially after my big sisters went away, giving us a spare bedroom. Usually young married couples joined us while the husband was getting his army or navy officer training.

Later on when the Americans joined in the war and were billeted in the town getting ready for D-Day, we used to have them to the house so my mother could give them "a good square meal". They were fun, but slowed down our Christmas dinner by eating only with their forks, not with knife and fork like we British do. There was Herbert E. Arnold from Memphis and Salvador A. Randazzo from Buffalo. The other odd thing was that Americans had only one middle initial. We British have several. They were very generous when they realized we were short of a lot of things. We used to ask the G.I.s, "Got any gum, chum?" and they would cheerfully give us chewing gum and "candy" (as they called our sweets) and souvenirs such as cap badges or uniform buttons.

They did talk in a funny way. My father's partner told about one who went into Boots the Chemist and asked for a roll of bath tissue. The girl behind the counter was baffled. Then she asked him if he meant toilet paper, and apparently he did. Then he asked for some soap. "Do you mean toilet soap?" she asked. "Oh no," he replied, "The kind you wash your face with."

American comics that made our English ones look tame came with the soldiers. I started a collection. At the beginning of the war I got *Chicks' Own*. My mother allowed me to take it to the Sunday service at the Congregational chapel to read during the sermon. Later when I was older I got *Beano* one week and *Dandy* the next; they used to come out every week before the war but then there wasn't enough paper. The American comics were really colorful with tough guy heroes like Superman who could jump over skyscrapers, and tough cops like Dick Tracy who had a two-way wrist radio, and athletic ladies with not many clothes on.

My sister Pat played the pipe organ in the chapel. That's because she had piano lessons and practiced. Sometimes it was embarrassing. Freddy Fuge, one of the big boys from the Sunday School, had to pump air for the organ by hand and if he got too slow or forgot, the music would gasp into silence. Pat would look around and signal frantically to him, hoping the congregation did not notice.

With so many evacuees coming we had enough playmates to form a gang. This meant that our parents were more lenient in allowing us to play further away than the second field, our previous limit. Now we were allowed to go through the railway underpass for the line to Looe and as far as the fourth field as long as there were several of us together. Having a gang meant that we could also make camps and have campfires. There was a place by the hedge in the fourth field where we dammed a stream and made a pond for our toy boats. We called our gang the "Chizzy-Chizzies". I don't remember why.

Once I showed our Chizzy-Chizzy camp to Uncle Victor. He was a colonel in the army, so he had a real revolver he let me hold when it was unloaded. I don't think he fought in many heroic battles, since he was only in the Education Corps, but he had a revolver anyway. I climbed up onto the hedge brandishing the revolver, but it was pretty heavy and I over balanced and fell into the pond. I got soaked and covered in mud but managed to hold the revolver out of the water. My mother was not pleased with the next load of laundry.

We had another visitor. That was one of the advantages of being in a war. People came to see us from all over the world. George Rawstron was my father's second cousin once removed or something like that. His parents had emigrated from Cornwall like a lot of "Cousin Jacks", as the Cornish emigrants were nicknamed. He was in the R.N.Z.N., the Royal New Zealand Navy. He was really good at unarmed combat.

I was small for my age, and a lot of the other boys were stronger than me. My sister gave me a book on unarmed combat that you couldn't borrow at the library, and cousin George taught me some good self-defense moves. I learned to throw someone over my shoulder when they tried to strangle from behind, and how to break their windpipe with the edge of my hand when they tried to strangle in front, but you had to be really careful with that. My favorites were the wrist burn and knocking my opponent to the ground with two fingers. I practiced that on John Wilkins, who was pretty nice about it, and then tried it with Vivian Denny, the bully at school. I didn't get bullied after that.

Our gang made another camp in the hedge between the first and second fields, next to a tall elm tree. The hedges were tall and wide, made of stone and earth. Hazel, wild plum, brambles and rose hips grew in them, so you could build good camps on top. My mother made blackberry and sloe jam from what I picked for her, which helped with the rations.

An old stone cattle shelter in the next field over was tumbling down, because the farmer wasn't using it any more. We borrowed sheets of corrugated iron from the roof, which probably made it tumble down a bit more. Anyway corrugated iron made splendid walls and a roof for our camp.

So long as we were careful our parents let us have campfires. They gave us potatoes to roast in the embers and salt to season them with. However, we were usually too hungry to wait for real embers. It seemed quicker to put the potatoes right into the flames. They got pretty black. When we thought they had been in long enough we got them out, cut them in half with our sheath knives (actually I just had a pocket knife; my mother thought a sheath knife was too dangerous) and put salt on them. We wished we had butter, but that was rationed. They were scrumptious anyway. Admittedly the salt got pretty black, because they were charcoaled on the outside and raw on the inside. We had strong teeth, and the flavor was delicious. Much more enjoyable than the hygienic grown-up meals our mothers took such pride in. We had campfires and baked potatoes as often as possible.

But then our gang had to take on a serious purpose. The Cahill gang lived on the other side of the field where the old barn was. The leader was Ronnie Cahill, and his second in command was David Tank. The Cahill gang was older than we were, rough, strong, and good at climbing trees. They were allowed to throw stones. Well, their fathers were away at the war and perhaps their mothers didn't know those rules. We were afraid they would attack and capture us, perhaps take over our camp or break it up, so we prepared.

The farmer used to feed his cows Brussels sprouts plants, and they were all over the first field. The fat stalks made splendid clubs, and unlike our wooden swords they wouldn't poke anybody's eyes out. (I actually had a wooden sword that I had made with Icelandic runes on it in charcoal, because I had just read *"The Hobbit".*) We armed ourselves to the teeth with the Brussels sprouts stumps, and when the Cahill gang finally rushed at us, we beat them off. We also ran away quite a lot so that they wouldn't get close enough to hit us when they threw stones. Sometimes with a stronger enemy you have to have a better plan and use superior tactics.

Soon Robin and Brian weren't allowed to come out to play. We were not sure why, but we heard their mothers crying, and they packed up their belongings and moved away. Their fathers weren't there to help. Not long after that, John and Jennifer went back to Plymouth because the air raids weren't as bad any more. There was still Jean Shearsmith. We had grown out of our pedal car and tricycle phase, and now our gang just wasn't the same. Actually, Jean's parents gave her a two-wheeler, and they kindly let me learn to ride it. But soon her father was transferred, and that was the end of Jean, too.

I had an adventure with Raymond Hocking. He was allowed to go even beyond the fourth field, and he had a pet ferret that he had trained and carried about in a burlap sack. Raymond could ride a bicycle, and he knew lots of swear words. When he needed to pee he didn't have to go home to use the bathroom; he just unbuttoned his fly and aimed himself at the hedge. And Raymond had a big sister who had a dark skinned baby boy, and she wasn't even married, so that was quite a miracle.

Raymond took me rabbiting. Our family used to eat a lot of wild rabbit, because with the rationing there were only a few ounces of butcher's meat a week, and that didn't go very far. Rabbit pie with parsley and pastry was my favorite. Once I made a pair of mittens with fur I had skinned off two rabbits, nailing them stretched out on a board and rubbing alum on them to cure them and olive oil to make them soft. I had meant to make fur gloves, but they were too difficult. My mother had to help me finish making the mittens.

Anyway, I went off rabbiting with Raymond Hocking. He said we should find a rabbit warren and put a snare or a net at all the burrows except one. The snares were like a lasso made of thin flexible wire with a noose. The nets had pegs to fasten them around the openings to the burrows. Then the ferret was put into the remaining hole, and it would chase the rabbits into the snares or nets. Raymond tied a piece of string around the ferret's muzzle in case it decided to eat the rabbit itself. Pretty soon we would have rabbit pie, or even several.

When he had everything ready, Raymond put the ferret into the remaining open hole. It quickly disappeared and we waited. We waited, and we waited. No rabbit. Actually, no ferret. Raymond Hocking began to look a bit anxious. He said he had spent a lot of time training that ferret and it was the only one he had. He didn't know if his father would buy him another.

We went on waiting. Still no rabbit. Still no ferret. At least it meant we didn't have to kill the rabbits that we caught. After a long while, probably at least five or six minutes, we gave up and walked home rather dejected. Raymond Hocking never took me rabbiting again.

Then the war led to new evacuees coming to Cornwall, just at a time when I was running short of playmates nearby. Teddy Spice came from London, and he was fun, although he had never seen cows before and thought they were horses with horns. He stayed with Miss Spence who was a teacher. We all admired him, because he had a hole in his skull covered by a metal plate. He wasn't allowed to climb trees.

Then there was Keith Baines. He came from Essex, near London. He stayed with the Misses Gill. There were a lot of unmarried ladies of about the same age who lived in Liskeard and who were very kind to the evacuee families, volunteering to take them into their homes. Many of them had once been engaged to be married but their fiancés had been killed in the Great War.

Being Cornish, we nicknamed Keith Baines "Beezer", and it stuck. There were several Beezers at our school. I remember Beezer Beamish, and I think there were a Beezer Brooks and a Beezer Brown. Beezer Baines and I became best friends. We made a good team, as I had a good imagination and Beezer was practical and knew a lot about science and how things were made.

Beezer and I got up to all kinds of projects. Once we built a canoe and launched it on the River Fowey when we went camping with a boys' group from the Wesleyan Chapel. Another time we went exploring in the fields. That was when I found my amazing cat Tigger. But those are stories for later.

We had an amazing stroke of luck when the Civil Defense decided to dump a huge pile of bricks in the field at the end of our lane. It was an untidy pile, so we decided to straighten it up. Before very long we had built an amazing fort, much better than the ones in the hedge with the rusty corrugated iron. The basic design was circular, like the Norman Restormel Castle near Lostwithiel, with a central bailey. The wall even had battlements. We built in embrasures with loopholes that we could poke our toy rifles through. I asked my father for some of the trellis from his garden, but he needed it for his Scarlet Runner beans. It was a formidable fort, and we had a great time training our admittedly small army to man it.

Unfortunately, the Civil Defense planned to build a Static Water Tank with the bricks, so we lost our fort. It too was circular, and they filled it with water to be used by the ARP with their stirrup pumps in case there were incendiary bomb attacks. They even covered it with chicken wire so that we couldn't swim in it, which was too bad. We thought building that water tank was a strategic mistake. If someone had just arranged for the Home Guard to man our fort and perhaps put some mortar between the bricks to keep it from falling down, it would have made a much better defense.

As it turned out, the ARP never had to use the Static Water Tank for the purpose for which it had been built. The war was going better, the air raids were less frequent, and we weren't nervous about being invaded any more.

Then there came good news indeed. The Allies brought Italy to its knees, and the Italians surrendered. That summer my father arranged with Reg Hocking for us to go on holiday at his farm, Tregrill, near Menheniot. We couldn't go as usual to our cottage in Polzeath on the north coast of Cornwall because the beach was covered with landmines, and barbed wire entanglements blocked access from our lane.

The Hockings had a boy, Colin, my age with two older sisters just like our family. The girls were Doreen and Peggy, and they taught me to feed the chickens, milk the cows, drive the tractor, and help with the harvest. I was ready to become a farmer when I grew up. A Land Girl was also at Tregrill as well as three Italian prisoners of war who came to help with the threshing. Since the Italians were enemies, I was afraid they would capture the tractor and escape. Would they shoot me? Actually, one who spoke a little English told Reg Hocking that they were relieved to stop fighting and just wanted to go home to their families when the war finally ended. One of them made me a bracelet with an identity disc with my name on it out of a piece of old saucepan, which was kind.

Then the BBC news announced that the invasion of France had culminated in the surrender of Germany. Everybody was relieved and happy. We all hoped the war in Asia would soon be over, too. But to our surprise there were no official plans in Liskeard for a celebration, even though the government in London had declared a VE Day to rejoice in the Allied Victory in Europe. We thought the Borough Council should have done something about it.

There weren't any fireworks because all the gunpowder had to be used for the war, so Beezer and I decided to have a bonfire in the big field opposite our house. It might be a good way of celebrating. I had a wooden wagon that my Uncle Dick had made for me, and we went around collecting old planks and scraps of wood and flammable things that people wanted to throw out.

We tried to get some of our friends from school and people from different parts of town to help. Mostly they thought our bonfire wouldn't amount to much, so they wouldn't join in. I think they felt they would look foolish if not much came of it. We asked the Liskeard Silver Band if they would come and play martial music, but they told us most of their bandsmen were away at the war, and anyway they could only play on official occasions.

So we plugged away. Soon the pile of wood grew much bigger than the kind of garden bonfire where people burned their dead leaves and branches. Then it got big enough that it could be seen from the road that went from the town down to the Great Western Railway station. People started bringing more wood to add to the pile, and by the time VE Day arrived it was about twelve feet in height and diameter and you had to throw wood really high to get it on the top.

The pile got so big that the mayor decided he would come and make a speech and officially light it himself, which he did when it got dark. Lots of people came not only from the town but also from a long way away, including sailors from Devonport and Land Girls (who helped on the farms) from their hostel at Pencubitt. Everybody sang *"God Save the King"* and then other patriotic songs like *"Rule Brittania"* and *"Land of Hope and Glory"* (although if you listened closely to what my sisters were singing it sounded more like land of soap and water). The celebrations went on late into the evening and even after I had to go to bed.

Just as everybody hoped, the attack on Japan was a success when the Americans dropped atomic bombs, and the whole war came to an end. The government declared VJ Day. This time the Borough Council decided they had better have a big celebration themselves, although they didn't ask Beezer and me to help. There were public teas at gathering places all over the town. People got out their Union Jacks, and the red, white and blue bunting they had displayed for the coronation of King George VI. They hung patriotic decorations from public buildings and private houses, from garden fences and from the tables for the public celebration teas. There were ministers and preachers at the teas saying grace and giving thanks for peace.

The best thing of all was that the church bells were allowed to ring again. Our parish church, St. Martin's, was at the top of the hill at the northeast part of the town, near Castle Hill. The bell ringers hadn't practiced, but nobody minded if a few notes were sour. It was enough that they were ringing again, because we had such great things to celebrate.

So at last the war was over. Amazingly, we kids somehow got through it all. Of course, in the country we didn't suffer the bombing that the people in the big cities went through. But we had to admit that we were scared most of the time: during air raids and especially when everybody thought there was going to be an invasion. I suppose we were deprived of a lot of stuff, but we got used to it and it wasn't that important. Although I must say that the first banana for Sunday breakfast since I was six, mashed up with sugar and Cornish clotted cream, was a huge treat.

There was also sadness that a lot of people from the town who had gone to help out the war effort would never come home again. The only thing you could do was keep a stiff upper lip and make the best of it throughout, which we children did with the help of our parents and friends. It *was* a good thing that the war was over, and I was glad that we won. It must be awful to lose. They said the Great War was the war to end all wars, but that did not work. Maybe this time the human race will learn to live in peace and collaborate to create prosperity and happiness for all, even if for no better reason than that wars will get worse and worse.

Kizzling Doney

I feel embarrassingly left out of conversations about unhappy childhoods and their devastating effects upon adult psychology. I was the youngest in the family, the only boy spoiled rotten by three mothers, if you count my two adoring much older sisters as sharing the maternal role. It was a perfect existence. I have no complaints.

There was one upsetting moment when I was four years old. I overheard my eldest sister Pam making a comment about me to our mother as she was helping her in the kitchen. It sounded disparaging and I rose indignantly to my own defense.

"I am NOT a kizzling doney child!"

My sister reassured me. "No, no, I was just saying to Mummy that with Pat and me being ten and thirteen years older than you, you are *equivalent to an only child.*"

Well, what was so bad about that? Pam and Pat gave me lots of attention. They took me on walks, showed me how to do things, helped me with projects, made me laugh, and I had plenty of playmates my age. Pam used to sit on my bed every night and sing *Red Sails in the Sunset* before I went to sleep.

I missed Pam when she went off to Cambridge, but she wrote amusing letters. I got a bit worried when she told me she had a boy friend; perhaps she would pay more attention to him than to me. She said he was very handsome and intelligent, and his name was Regibald Archibald Jeribald. Pat said she thought Pam was just teasing me, and I shouldn't take her seriously.

About that time I spent three months in Copenhagen with my mother. She needed to go to Denmark for specialized medical treatment that was not available in England. I had her undivided attention except when my father took us over and later came to bring us back. The North Sea crossing from Harwich was stormy, and my mother and I were seasick most of the way.

I thought the food in Denmark was disgusting and smelled foreign, so I looked forward to jam and clotted cream and the saffron bun my father promised me when he came for our return trip. There was a young woman in the rooms next to ours where we were staying, an aspiring opera star. She practiced shrill scales and arpeggios hour after hour, day after day. My father telephoned and said I should just stuff an onion in her mouth.

After we got home to England my parents decided it was high time for me to go to school. I was close to the compulsory school age of five, so at the start of the new school year in September my mother dragged me on the short walk, about a mile, to the small private school in the center of Liskeard.

Fortunately, we didn't encounter any of my friends on the way. It would have been embarrassing, because the full name of the school was Highwood House School for Girls. My sisters had gone there, but I did not want to go. A few boys were admitted to kindergarten and stayed until they were old enough at ten to go on to the secondary school. Older pupils were girls only. I imagined that only sissy boys went to the school, and I did not want to be perceived as one. However, I was soon to learn that there was a nasty little tough among my schoolmates.

Memories of the school were brought back during my recent book tour of Cornwall. I gave a talk at the Liskeard Book Shop on Barras Street, just a couple of buildings along from Highwood House. John Rapson, a nephew of the headmistress, was in the audience and shared professional photographs he had taken of me as a boy.

Miss Rapson was a precise no-nonsense teacher as was her companion, Miss Wilkes. The school was in their house. They were both formidable disciplinarians with acerbic tongues. To start the day each of us had fifteen conduct marks, which were whittled away with each passing infraction of studiousness or behavior. In the first form we sat in rows on long benches attached to long wooden desks. There were grooves along the top to stop our pens and pencils rolling down and ink wells at every place. There were individual lids so that we could keep our pencil boxes, exercise books, pen wipers and spare nibs inside. There were still one or two slates in the room but Miss

Rapson had decided to modernize and provide her pupils with exercise books and paper.

I was a good little boy and hated getting into trouble, sailing through the day with conduct marks intact. I paid attention in class and avoided the sarcastic scolding that some pupils endured. I memorized the multiplication tables, right up to twelve times. My sisters helped me practice spelling, so I did well in the daily tests and quickly learned to read. Even though my handwriting was not very tidy and abundantly decorated with ink blots, like my fingers, I was careful to make the loops upright. I hated drawing and painting, and I had trouble not going over the lines. Fortunately, we boys were not made to do needlework like the girls.

Every day there was recess. When it was wet and cold, Miss Wilkes would make us play singing and rhyming action games indoors. I remember the one about the bells of London's churches.

> *Oranges and lemons,*
> *Say the bells of St. Clement's.*
> *You owe me five farthings,*
> *Say the bells of St. Martin's.*
> *When will you pay me?*
> *Say the bells of Old Bailey.*
> *When I grow rich,*
> *Say the bells of Shoreditch.*

Pamela Raymont, a farmer's daughter who lived in the country, kept choosing me as a partner for the games, which was pretty embarrassing, and I avoided her. She was pretty with blonde hair, blue eyes and a beautiful pink and white complexion. After we both went to the secondary school, she blossomed, and I wished I had paid her more attention, but by then it was too late.

Vivian Denny was the son of one of the local butchers, and he got rough when it came to the bit about *"Along came a chopper to chop off her head!"* On fine days recess was outside. There was a big upper playground for the girls and a smaller playground for the boys. Vivian Denny always wanted to play rough games, like fighting, and wrestling. He was a lot stronger than I and always beat me but there wasn't much I could do about it. He always found me even though I tried to avoid him. Telling Miss Wilkes would be sneaking. My father said I should punch him on the jaw, but I was afraid he would punch me back harder. I would have to think of a winning strategy.

Most of the time school was enjoyable. One term my sister Pat came to teach part time while she was waiting to start her training as a physiotherapist. She tried to be strict with me, so that the other children would not think I was her favorite, but she could not help being nice. And once every term there was a special treat.

The whole school was invited into the private part of the house to sit in the big front hall, and Miss Rapson would show us her museum. Her father had been a Methodist missionary in Africa, and she would tell us stories about converting the heathen and persuading them to give up being cannibals. I thought I would like to be a missionary but then learned it was dangerous and poorly paid. Anyway, Miss Rapson had a marvelous collection of things her father had brought back from Africa, and we loved looking at them and holding them. There were masks, costumes, sculptures, primitive art, assegais (sharp short stabbing spears), shields made of rhinoceros hide, knives, elephants' tusks, stuffed animal heads, beads, pots, letters, and old photographs of missionaries.

We learned a lot at Highwood House. The pupils certainly got a solid grounding in the three Rs, and in learned manners and good behavior. We learned about the world and developed an interest in geography. Those were innocent days. It never occurred to us to wonder exactly what were the living arrangements for these two spinster ladies living all their lives in the same house. Our parents never brought up the subject. We just assumed it was convenient and perfectly natural. Sometimes when we are nostalgic for the good old days it is that kind of innocence that I most miss.

The Best Cat in the World

When I was a little boy in Cornwall I wanted to be a veterinarian. I loved animals. At the time I didn't have any, because my parents didn't think I was old enough to look after pets. They didn't want to take on the responsibility.

The animals I loved most were horses. That was because my Granfer used to tell me stories about the horse business he had when he was a young man. My favorite hobby became cutting horse pictures out of magazines and newspapers and sticking them in a scrapbook. Soon I became enthusiastic about having a pony for my first pet.

The drawback was that we lived in the town and had nowhere to keep a pony. Giving that some thought, I tried to convince my father that we could keep my pony on our back lawn and turn his tool shed into a stable. Argument turned to disappointment when he said the lawn was far too small, and there wouldn't be enough grass to feed a hungry animal. He added that he needed his tool shed for tools.

Fred Martin the milkman had a pony and trap that he used for delivering milk. I asked him if I could keep my pony with his. "Company for your pony," I said. Fred replied that he was too busy to look after another animal. My father asked a neighbor, Mr. Blee, if I could ride his pony that used to compete in gymkhanas, sort of sports meets for horses. He said she was too frisky for a small boy like me. I had to accept that I wouldn't be getting a pony any time soon.

My second choice was a dog. I started research and borrowed books from the library. Various breeds and the special purposes for which they had been developed opened new dreams. I studied manuals on the sicknesses and health problems of dogs and how to take care of them, learning how many things could go wrong. I was fascinated by books on how to train dogs, everything from obedience to retrieving, from showing to hunting, from pointing to parlor tricks. I decided that what I really wanted was a pure bred, pedigreed Irish

Red Setter. It would cost a lot, so I started saving my pocket money and dropping hints for the next couple of Christmases and birthdays.

I imagined that I would train my dog to find pheasants for me to shoot when I was old enough to have a shotgun, and that it would become a field trial champion. There were a couple of minor problems. There were no pheasants where we lived. And I hadn't heard of any field trials for Irish Setters nearby. Not letting that curb my enthusiasm, I started cutting out pictures of Irish Setters from magazines and newspapers and pasting them in a new scrapbook that I kept next to the one on horses.

A week or two later there was a pet show in our town. I went to it with my best friend "Beezer" Baines, the evacuee from London. Seeking out the Irish Red Setters, I found to my surprise and disappointment there weren't any. There Foxhounds, Wire Haired Fox Terriers, Border Collies, and Cocker Spaniels. After all my reading, I felt like an expert on all of the breeds. However, I remained loyal to the Irish Setter, even though I knew I wasn't going to get any kind of puppy at that point in time.

Many different kinds of pets were shown. I knew my mother disapproved of gambling, but nevertheless I spent some of my pocket money on a lottery ticket, though I had never won anything before. To my surprise, I won six baby rabbits! I tried to persuade my mother to let me keep them. Breeding rabbits for their fur and making gloves and waistcoats and other useful things would earn me pocket money. Mummy said I couldn't keep them, and anyway we didn't have a rabbit hutch or anywhere to keep them, *and* they would get smelly. I knew better by then than to ask for my father's tool shed.

The next Saturday, Beezer and I went exploring in the fields behind my house and heard a squeaking sound coming from a thick hedge. I climbed up into it, trying not to get scratched. As I got closer to the sound, there in the middle of a hazel thicket was hidden a nest with eight tortoiseshell colored kittens in it. They were crying for their mother. They looked about six weeks old, ready for weaning. I thought I'd better rescue at least one of them, and picked out the prettiest. Just then, the mother returned in a high old state.

She was a feral cat that we'd often seen running around the fields, hunting mice and birds. She had lost one of her front legs in a rabbit gin but still managed to move around well. Her disability didn't stop her scratching and biting. My hands and arms were scratched to ribbons, but I was determined not to give up on my rescue.

I took the kitten home, hoping that my mother would allow me to keep him. In the end, the softness of her heart was too much for the hardness of her head. Before I could even enter my plea, the kitten was in a round basket on a soft towel lapping at a saucer of milk. She put the basket in the conservatory at the back of our house with a high window open for ventilation. I fell asleep that night with triumphant dreams of the world's first obedience trained circus cat.

Imagine my disappointment and mystification when I went down to the conservatory the next morning to find the basket empty and the kitten gone. Where was it? We could only imagine that the three-legged mother had somehow jumped through the open high window, picked up her kitten by the scruff of its neck and jumped out again. I was not allowed to skip breakfast, but as soon as I could, I set off for the nest in the hazel hedge. The mother cat was off hunting so I could count the kittens, and sure enough there were eight. I carefully picked out "my" kitten (I *think* I got the right one) and hurried home before the mother reappeared. Safe at last!

Well, not quite. It turned out that my father was kept awake half the previous night by the kitten's mewling. His enthusiasm for an enlarged family was at a low ebb when fate intervened. My Aunt Betty called in to visit. She was not a favorite with my father, who thought she was bossy and interfering. True to form she picked up the kitten, to pronounce as to its health, gender and suitability. It hissed at her and scratched her hand! That won my father's heart, and the kitten stayed; as it turned out, for the next thirteen years.

Now an official family member, the kitten needed a name. His stripes made him look like a tiger so, with what at the time I thought was a stroke of originality, I named him "Tigger". (Actually, I think it might have been my sister Pat's idea. She had given me the Christopher Robin books for my birthday.)

The work of training began in earnest. It turned out that Tigger did not think much of obedience and shared no ambition for running away to star in a circus. However, he was motivated by food, and his favorite was fish. My mother bought fish from Mr. Minards, who came up by train from the nearby fishing port, bringing cod and mackerel and pilchards in an old pram, a large sort of baby carriage. So Tigger's meals consisted of fish heads Mr. Minards had cut off when trimming fish for other customers. I would boil them up in an old saucepan. Tigger could smell them from miles away, which was no trick. It didn't take special cat nostrils, the stink was awful.

Soon, it got to the point that when Tigger heard me rattling the old saucepan, he would come running, looking for fish. Then I started calling his name when I rattled the saucepan. Soon, when I called "Tigger Tigger Tigger TIGGERRRR!" he would come running whether I was cooking fish or rattling the saucepan or not. Tigger became the world's best cat at coming when his name was called. Training had started.

I was generally a good little boy, mostly obedient. This included going to bed early when I was told. But I wasn't allowed to read or have Tigger in bed. These are rules I found had no merit. When my parents came to kiss me good night, I hid my flashlight under my pillow and hoped that Tigger wouldn't meow audibly from under the bedclothes. Keeping Tigger near me was worth risking my parents' wrath which wasn't often terrible.

I was allowed to take Tigger with me when we went to stay on a farm called Tregrill for our summer vacation. He was put in his round basket, and the lid was closed so he wouldn't jump out of the open window of the car and get hurt. He couldn't see the pretty countryside as we drove on our journey; his complaints were more about being a captive than being deprived of the view.

When we arrived at Tregrill I took him in his basket up to my room, and made sure the door and windows were closed before I let him out. I didn't want him to escape and get chased by the sheepdogs in the farmyard or run off and get lost. I had read that if you smear butter on a cat's paws, by the time he licks it off he will be used to his new surroundings and won't run away. So that's what I did, using delicious fresh butter that the farmer's wife had made herself. That night he slept in my room, and I think my mother secretly knew that he was hiding in my bed and didn't mind.

The next morning I took him down for breakfast and let him go exploring in the farmhouse. In the afternoon I took him for a walk in the farmyard. He came when I called, just like he always did. I took him out on an expedition again that evening, but when I called he didn't come. I called and called. I looked everywhere. No Tigger. I was upset and not comforted when my mother assured me he would probably come back in the morning after a night out hunting mice.

He didn't come back the next day or the day after that. I looked everywhere and called and called. I even boiled up some stinky fish heads and put the pan outside where he could smell them, calling Tigger, Tigger, Tigger. No Tigger. I tried to be brave, but it was awful.

That weekend my father went back into town to check into his office and make sure our house was all right. I looked forward to his return because we always had a "good yarn", as he used to say. When he arrived there was a big smile on his face and a bulge under his jacket. It was Tigger! I swear there was a smile on Tigger's face too when he saw me.

That amazing cat had somehow found his way for miles across country to our home. Yet on the way out to the farm, he had been shut inside his basket unable to see out. How on earth did he do it? Tigger truly was the best cat in the world.

I loved the rest of our stay at the farm. I drove the tractor, helped with the harvest, stooked the sheaves of wheat, built the rick, collected the eggs, fed the calves, milked the cows by hand, and rode "'Ecker" the old chestnut cob bare back. All I wanted to be when I grew up was a farmer. Well, maybe a veterinarian too.

My parents knew how much I loved animals and especially how much I wanted a dog. My birthday was coming up, and they said if I was really responsible about cooking Tigger's fish and feeding him regularly for a whole month, then they would consider my getting my own puppy. Since I had already been to the dog show and read books from the library about all the different breeds, I knew that the Irish Red Setter was my favorite. I wanted a pure bred from a good strain, because the books said that would be the best kind of dog for finding and retrieving birds and also for showing. I was excited.

The next Monday I went up to the cattle market to get some fish heads from Mr. Minards. In a box next to his cart he had a litter of playful little puppies. I ran all the way home and told my mother about them. She said I could have one. I think she may have privately been relieved, since the puppy would be a lot less expensive than a pure bred Irish Red Setter. So I took the money back to Mr. Minards and chose a lively little fellow with a black patch over one eye. I called him Mack and carried him proudly home. My sister Pat told me that he was from a very good breed, the Black and White Sheepdog, which made me proud, although I had never seen a Black and White Sheepdog in my books and suspected she might be teasing. Tigger watched us from a corner, not sure just what to do about this new member of the family.

I decided to train Mack to become a champion sheepdog. I got more books from the library and read all about the sheepdog trials that were held at agricultural shows. The main thing you had to learn was to whistle the different signals. Mack thought it was a grand idea, and started practicing by rounding Tigger up into a flock, since we didn't have any sheep. Tigger thought his part of the training was to scratch Mack on the muzzle whenever he got too enthusiastic. Herding Tigger turned out to be quite a challenge, and I must say if Mack had succeeded there is no doubt he would have become a world champion with straightforward sheep. But it was not to be. Sadly, Mack got very sick with distemper when he was only six months old and died. I was so sad that I didn't get another dog for a long time.

While I was at the library, I also borrowed some books about pigeon breeding and racing. This seemed really interesting, and I asked if my parents if I could get some pigeons from Mr. Sweet, the woodsman who worked at the Duchy Woods. They said yes almost right away, and my father had one of Uncle Dick's carpenters build a pigeon loft in our back yard. It had a "trap" with swinging rods that kept the pigeons in so they couldn't escape, but it also let them get back into their nests after they had been flying around outside. I started out with three pairs of racing pigeons. They were beautiful with sleek feathers and iridescent breasts.

I trained them to come when they were called. Keeping their corn in a tin can, I rattled it at feeding time, and they would come to the loft just like Tigger when he heard me banging the pot of fish. I thought I would train them to become champion racers and even fly in the famous thousand-mile race from Rome, competing against famous pigeons owned by the Queen of England and Sir Gordon Richards, the champion jockey. Or maybe they could learn to carry important secret messages attached to their legs. According to the book, you started their "homing" training when they were sitting on eggs on their nests, because then they were anxious to get home. You took one of the pair in a basket a short way away, gradually increasing the distance until they could "home" from quite a long way away.

I took them to the railway station, where often there were lots of special baskets containing pigeons released to race back to distant cities. When I looked inside the empty baskets I saw eggs. The stationmaster said they would be thrown away. He suggested I take them home and give them to my pigeons to hatch. Maybe I would breed a fast flyer with amazing endurance from a champion strain!

Could this be true? Would my own pigeons really hatch a strange egg? Then the first one hatched. His little head moved quickly on his neck when he took pigeon's milk from his step-parents' beaks. I called him Riki-Tiki-Tavi, after the mongoose in the Rudyard Kipling story about Sabu the Elephant Boy in India. His name sounded like the "arikatoo" cooing sound pigeons make. I had worried about Tigger's hunting instincts where my pigeons were concerned, so I decided to train him to become friends with them, starting with Riki-Tiki-Tavi. Soon I had Tigger in my lap taking fish from one hand and Riki-Tiki-Tavi on my shoulder taking corn from my other hand. Tigger was an amazing cat.

When I was thirteen, my parents decided I should go away to boarding school. It was a sad moment when I had to leave Tigger and my pigeons; it at least gave me something to write about in my obligatory weekly letter home. And I soon got busy at school and missed them less. But then there was a nasty surprise. I got a letter from my parents with the news that Tigger had disappeared. I was devastated, and became homesick.

Eventually my first term was over, and with excitement I took the train home. My parents met me at the station and we headed home for lunch. We had an old sofa in our breakfast room, where I often sat and read while my mother was working in the kitchen. Imagine my surprise and joy to see Tigger curled up in my favorite seat! He jumped on my lap and purred while I stroked him under his chin.

Tigger celebrated Christmas with us with some turkey tidbits and stayed home for the rest of the school holidays. But after my first week back at school I got what would become the familiar letter from my parents. Tigger had disappeared again. This time I wasn't sad. I just thought what an amazing cat he was to go off adventuring on his own while I was away. I knew he would come home again when I did. The next holidays, when I arrived home and looked at his favorite seat on the old sofa, there he was washing his face and purring away. This happened over and over the whole time I was away at school. He would never have anything much to do with the rest of my family.

When I left school and went to the university, Tigger would still show up when I came home for vacations and disappear the rest of the time. Then one vacation I brought my girl friend home to meet my parents. Sometimes when we were alone she would sit on my lap. Tigger stalked off with his tail in the air and a disgusted look on his face. When we became engaged to be married, it made things all right with Tigger. From then on he would jump on top of her lap and sit there with both of us, purring happily.

After finishing university we were married, and I started a job, not living at home after that. I never did get to be a veterinarian. But I've gone on loving animals. Tigger stayed with my parents. He was getting old, and I felt he would be disturbed by moving to a new home in a strange town, and might run away forever and get lost. He didn't stay home much with my parents. He would check in every now and again to see what was going on, maybe accepting some food without showing much gratitude. He pretty much fended for himself. My parents' letters mentioned him less and less. Eventually, he stopped showing up. I imagine he decided to become the best cat in heaven.

I never really meant to get a cat. But Tigger was amazing. I loved him so much. He was a one-man cat, which I secretly enjoyed. I've never had a personal cat since. I'm glad Tigger and I had each other and I will always remember him.

Constitution of an Ox

My favorite aunt was Aunty Betty. There were lots of aunts to choose from and they were all pretty nice and inclined to spoil a small nephew. My mother was one of ten children, five boys and five girls. Like many of their generation two were spinsters, their fiancés killed in the Great War.

My father had one sister, Hilda, who was always interested in what was going on and told stories about our Hoskin ancestors, but she lived a long way away in Wadebridge where my father was born. My Granfer lived in Wadebridge too. I used to love holding his hand and walking around the town while he told me stories of olden times, especially about horses. We didn't often go to Wadebridge though, and when we did we hired a car and driver to travel the twenty miles. Rarely done. However, at least they all lived in Cornwall.

Granfer's hands were strong from his days driving a coach and four. Hanging in his front hall was a whip with a long lash. He told me how he used to "tickle the ears" of the leading horses to get them to speed up. Next to the whip was his long copper coach horn that he taught me to play; it sounded out the coach coming and going. After he died the coach horn came to me, and it is still one of my proudest possessions, one which my own children and grandchildren love to blow on New Year's Eve. When Granfer was a young man, he had a horse and carriage business, Derry & Hoskin, at the end of the bridge down by the River Camel.

Granfer had grey horses for weddings and black horses and a hearse for funerals. He also had heavy draft horses and wagons. Proud of having driven William Ewart Gladstone throughout Cornwall on his famous Midlothian election campaign, he told how the great Liberal defeated Benjamin Disraeli and become prime minister. Granfer's Dalmatian Flo ran behind the back axle of the coach and slept in the stable with the horses to keep watch over them. My father learned to ride before he could walk, sitting on his pony with its reins linked between his father's and his Granfer's riding on either side of him.

But Aunty Betty was my favorite. Part of the reason was that she always gave me £5 at the beginning of every school term. That was in the days when £5 notes were bigger than £1 or 10 shilling notes and printed on one side of crisp white paper, the kind called banknote. £5 was worth so much then that whenever a note changed hands you signed your name on the back. My mother said that Aunty Betty was comfortably off and could well afford it. She had been widowed twice and both of her husbands left her money.

She had a stepson with one of them, Uncle Rodgy. He was a retired tea planter from India, a bachelor, and lived in rooms with Mrs. May at the end of Manley Terrace. A gimpy leg forced him to walk with a cane, but he made it down every day to The Stag just before lunch. My mother said he drank. He was a dry old stick and used to tell me stories with a raspy smoke-rough voice. He gave me some serious advice. "Don't marry for money, my son, but be near where 'tis."

Aunty Betty was a tough old bird and made her feelings known, especially when I slipped into the habit of seeing her only three times a year: once at the beginning of every term. She had retired as matron of the Bristol Royal Infirmary where she disciplined the young nurse probationers at the hospital through sheer terror. She was still in charge when my big sister Pat went there to qualify as a physiotherapist. Pat admired her. The war was on and during the blackout Aunty Betty used to walk her home at night through the rougher city streets, protecting her from the young servicemen keeping themselves cheerful with too much beer.

Before we moved, we lived next to Aunty Betty. My Uncle Dick built our houses. My father thought Aunty Betty was bossy, although he wisely kept that to himself. The nice thing about her house was that it had concrete paths. These were much better for my little red pedal car than our gravel paths, so I spent a lot of time there. She lived alone upstairs and rented the ground floor to a retired farmer and his wife. When I visited her she would give me a Jacob's Cream Cracker with butter, scraped thin because it was rationed.

I especially enjoyed sitting at her front window looking out and waiting for Ernie Penna to arrive. Poor old Ernie didn't have good jobs because he wasn't right in the head and couldn't speak clearly. He was a well-known local character. Every day he would walk down to the railway station to pick up the evening newspapers from Plymouth and come back up Station Road with them in a canvas bag slung over his shoulder. He also carried a long pole and lit the gas lamps along the street as he went. Ernie would call out, "Eeran Errol". If you were in the know, you knew that was Evening Herald. With a penny from Aunty Betty, I would run out across the street to buy her paper from Ernie.

Getting around town was accomplished by walking or running, sometimes both; it was no more than a mile or so down to the railway station or up into the town or to school, and in those days one didn't even wonder whether it was safe for a small boy to be out alone. It was. The "scout's pace" was a way of traveling long distances without tiring, alternately walking and running fifty paces each. It was one of the ideas General Robert Baden-Powell brought back from the Boer War in South Africa when he founded the Boy Scouts.

My favorite way to travel was in Fred Martin's pony and trap. Fred was the milkman and he would pick me up on my way home from school most days, deliver milk to my grandmother and then on to my mother where he would drop me off in time for lunch. Fred kept his pony in my grandmother's field. She said that he drank. He had big jowls and a big red nose. My grandmother didn't really approve of my riding with someone who drank, but Fred was always nice to me, and it was fast.

Some interesting "furriners" lived in Liskeard. Mr. and Mrs. Wilson were near neighbors and came from Yorkshire, way up country. She was a teacher and he was a chemist. Mr. Wilson was a brilliant mathematician and could multiply two six-digit numbers in his head. He worked for the nearby explosives manufacturer, advising mining engineers on placing explosives for the safest and most effective rock fall in order to get at the tin and copper deep in the mines.

The Wilsons had a black Labrador called Gyp, and he made me want one of my own. There wasn't much meat spared for dogs, so I used to take our bones to the Wilsons for Gyp, and they let me play with him. They were quietly proud of their son. He too was a brilliant mathematician and after Oxford became an economist and went into politics as a Socialist after the war. He rose to be President of the Board of Trade, the youngest cabinet minister since William Pitt the Younger. Later, Harold Wilson became Prime Minister.

It was just a month or two after the war ended when the Labour Party withdrew from the coalition government. Parliament was dissolved in June, and there was a general election. Everyone was excited. The election marked a return to normal peacetime activities. People expected Winston Churchill to lead his Conservative party, the Tories, to a big win in gratitude for his inspiring war leadership.

I looked forward to taking part, maybe actually campaigning. Our family was Liberal and actively involved, of which more anon. Liberal politics had a lasting influence on my life. My father particularly admired the great Isaac Foot who had been our M.P. before the war. Mr. Foot's father had been a carpenter. Isaac educated himself and became a lawyer, a solicitor, in the nearby city of Plymouth, although he lived in Cornwall. He was a student of Oliver Cromwell, a Methodist lay preacher, and an ardent teetotaler. After being lord mayor, he was elected to the House of Commons and rose to being the Secretary for India in the last Liberal government.

Isaac Foot had five sons, and every morning at breakfast each son had to make a one-minute speech. That practice stood them in good stead. They all went to Oxford and three became presidents of the Union, the debating society. Hugh went into the Colonial Service and triumphed as the last Governor of Cyprus. His brothers said he loved dressing up in fancy uniforms. However, he settled the intractable Cypriot civil war between the Greeks and the Turks. His reward was a peerage, and he retired as Lord Caradon, named after the Cornish tin mine near his father's home, Pencrebar.

Dingle Foot went into law and was elected M.P. for North Cornwall. After the death of his father, and indeed virtually the Liberal Party, Dingle joined the Labour party, became the Solicitor General and was knighted. John was the Liberal Candidate for Southeast Cornwall in the 1945 election, joined the family solicitor's practice and later became Baron Foot.

Michael was Isaac's secret favorite. He was strongly anti-fascist and a radical socialist, taking his father's progressive politics a big step further. As a young man he was a hard-hitting and widely read London journalist. Michael Foot was elected M.P. for Devonport and became an effective and passionate orator in the House of Commons. He rose to become the parliamentary leader of the Labour Party and would have become prime minister had Labour won the election. True to his egalitarian principles, he refused the peerage offered him upon retirement.

The youngest son Christopher led a private life with the family firm of solicitors. His reputation is that of a warm man, an able lawyer and of the highest integrity.

When I became president of the Oxford University Liberal Club and was charged with putting together a program, I invited both Dingle and John Foot to come and speak. Both were kind enough to accept. John gave me a speaking tip. I had been asked to be a paper speaker at the Union and was a bit nervous about introducing the debate. John told me to soften up the critical audience with humor and gave me his father's favorite joke. As I later stood at the dispatch box in the debating chamber, I intoned with what I trust passed as originality, "One must not think that the Church of England is the Tory party at prayer." Appreciative chuckles reverberated through the debating hall.

One of my proudest possessions is the cut crystal fruit bowl given me as a wedding present by Isaac Foot. These memories were in my mind when I visited Liskeard during my recent book tour for my Cornish historical novel, *The Miner & the Viscount,* with my daughter Sarah. Then one of our daily synchronicities happened. Being from Boulder, she was tickled to see a car with Colorado license plates. That afternoon I gave a talk at the Liskeard Public Library, complete with a Cornish cream tea. The enthusiastic librarian introduced herself as Tracee Foot. She turned out to be the owner of the car.

"Foot?" I asked. Her husband proved to be Jesse Foot, grandson of the late Michael Foot. Tracee and Jesse met at university in Colorado and decided to settle in Cornwall after they married. We arranged to have tea the next day, a delightful opportunity to get to know them and learn of Jesse's political ambitions, apparently a family trait.

As I mentioned, my first campaign was supporting John Foot in 1945. He and his supporters had to move fast with the campaign lasting only three weeks. As a boy I was more enthusiastic than valuable, but my biggest sister Pam was fantastic. When she was at Cambridge (which we Oxonians disparaged as a technical college in the fens!), like Michael Foot, she strayed to the left of traditional Cornish liberalism. She had been impassioned by the Spanish Civil War when Cambridge undergraduates had fought against Franco's fascists. For a while she thought that Karl Marx made a lot of sense, a not unusual view in those days.

Pam campaigned for John Foot all over the countryside, warming up the crowds in the towns and villages with eloquence, erudition, passion and humor. She was particularly effective in attacking the Tory candidate, Commander Douglas Marshall, R.N. He was a novice and not yet an imaginative speaker. His speech was a variation of three repeated themes delivered in a plummy accent that my sister parodied with barbed wit. "I believe in a strong navy, a strong army, and a strong air force. Furthermore, I am convinced of this country's need for a strong air force, and a strong army as well as a strong navy. To which, emphatically, I would add . . ." And so forth.

I should not be too hard on Marshall. He did get elected. Later when he came to speak to the Conservative Club at Oxford he was kind enough to invite me to dinner. I seized the opportunity to ask him for advice on a political career. "Commander Marshall, what is the secret of success as a Member of Parliament?" Without hesitation he replied, "Constitution of an ox, Richard my boy, constitution of an ox."

On one memorable evening during the campaign Commander Marshall gave his familiar speech from the balcony of the Conservative Club at the end of Fore Street in the center of Liskeard, just below the Guildhall with its imposing clock tower. My sister Pam was part of the crowd listening below. The crowd was hardly spellbound by the oratory and grew restive. Among the distinguished supporters on the balcony behind the candidate Pam spotted none less than Ernie Penna, with his bag of newspapers slung over his shoulder. She also spotted an opportunity. She started a chant, "We want Ernie, we want Ernie!" The crowd picked it up. "We want Ernie, we want Ernie, we want Ernie," drowning the speaker who simply gave up.

When a grinning Ernie stepped forward and spoke in his incomprehensible garble the crowd hollered their greeting. Commander Marshall never regained his composure or control of the crowd. The meeting broke up. John Foot's supporters sensed victory.

Unfortunately, however, a Liberal victory was not to be. On election day, July fifth, the socialist tabloid newspaper *The Daily Mirror* ran a sensational front page with a graphic of a fist brandishing a revolver and the headline "Whose finger on the trigger?" This stoked voter fear of the audacious and venturesome personality of the wartime prime minister Winston Churchill. His Conservatives were defeated, Labour won in a landslide and the Liberal Party was in tatters. Cornwall once again ran against the national tide; a Labour interloper split the radical vote and the Conservative won.

Aunty Betty, Uncle Rodgy, the Wilsons, the Foots, my sisters, Douglas Marshall, Ernie Penna. What characters! What a boyhood!

Boatbuilders

My best wartime friend was "Beezer" Baines, the evacuee from near London. He knew more about living in a city than I. But I knew much more about living in the country than he did. Most of the evacuees from London thought we country kids were pretty slow and kind of ignorant. We called them townies, uppity and know-it-all. What fun it was when they were shown up as not so smart after all.

Beezer was different: wanted to get to know you and would share interesting things about himself. He had a command of science, inventions, astronomy, world records, and weapons of war.

From Beezer I learned the different types of aircraft in the Battle of Britain but couldn't match his ability to tell the makes of German bombers attacking the nearby naval dockyard by the sounds of their engines. He knew how barrage balloons and searchlights worked and what disguises the German paratroopers would wear if an invasion came. I took his advice and watched out for storm troopers dressed up as nuns.

What I liked best about Beezer was that he didn't show off about how much he knew. He just shared it. I had some of the same interests and different ones too. When we went to get books out of the library, he would choose science or inventions. I chose animals or adventures or foreign lands.

His interest in collecting train engine numbers got us going down to the railway station to write down in our notebooks the numbers of the locomotives as they steamed past us pulling trains. Eventually we bought booklets that listed all of the locomotives in the Great Western Railway, and we marked off the ones we had seen. We tried to collect all of the numbers in a particular class. The great King class was too heavy to cross Brunel's bridge over the River Tamar into Cornwall, so we never got those.

Beezer explained that the locomotive type was described by the wheel arrangement. An engine with four small front wheels, six big driving wheels and two small rear wheels would be a 4-6-2, for example. The big ones pulled separate tenders carrying water and coal for making the steam that powered them. The small ones had built-in compartments for coal and water. If the water tanks were on the sides of the boiler it was called a "saddle tank". We soon got a good collection, and it became time for a new hobby.

I had joined a group called the "Pathfinders". It was formed by a local Methodist minister and was something like the Boy Scouts but not affiliated with a large international organization. We learned knots, did gymnastics, played games, and had a workshop where we could do wood working. Then our leader announced an exciting plan. Next summer we were to go camping for a week on a farm by the River Fowey.

Beezer and I decided it would be great fun to build a canoe for the trip. We really wanted it to be all wood, but my mother wasn't very keen on our taking up her kitchen for hours on end to use steam from her kettle to bend long planks of wood for the curved sides. She had become proud of her kitchen since my father bought her a refrigerator and a washing machine with rotary ironing and wringing attachments (the first in Liskeard) to make housework easier. Mrs. McShane still came on Mondays to help with the washing, and Fred Martin delivered fresh milk every day, so my sisters remember that she kept paper bags from the grocer in the refrigerator to use again.

Since wooden planking was out of the question, we thought of using birch bark like Hiawatha, the hero in Tennyson's famous poem about Native Americans. We made axe heads out of slate. Hiawatha used flint, but there wasn't any flint near where we lived. The only birch trees we found were too small and the bark split when we tried to peel it off the trunks. And trying to tie willow twigs together with vines to make a frame was more difficult than it looked. The twigs split and the vines snapped. We thought Hiawatha must have been skillful and admired what his people could do with primitive tools.

Our solution was to make a simple oblong canoe with a frame of wood covered in canvas. The frame was eight feet long and two and a half feet wide, big enough to hold one person. We built it in the

Pathfinders' workshop out of scraps of wood we scrounged from my uncle's builder's yard. We measured the wood carefully and sawed and chiseled and drilled it with hand tools. Getting the finished frame out of the workshop was cumbersome, but we managed.

When we went to buy canvas we found it was more expensive than our combined pocket money, so we decided to use a lightweight shelf fabric instead. It turned out not to be waterproof, which is a disadvantage when building a boat. But we went ahead and used the fabric and waterproofed it with paint. Since the paint was also expensive, my uncle let us have a half-used can of green oil paint he didn't need, so that problem was solved.

We painted the outside of the canoe and as much of the inside as we could reach, just to be safe. Since it took more paint than we expected there was none left to finish the inside, but the bottom was covered, so we felt the critical part would be waterproof. The fabric soaked up almost all the paint, and that made the canoe kind of heavy.

Next we had to come up with a name. The green color looked very smart. So my Latin teacher, who also knew Spanish, suggested we call our craft *El Verde Diablo Pequeño*, "The Little Green Devil." We thought that had a nice ring to it.

Being methodical, I said it was time to test our canoe on our friend Nigel Cummings' pond before we risked launching it on the fast flowing River Fowey. Beezer replied that he had been reading about Sir Malcolm Campbell and his famous speedboat *Bluebird*. He had recently set a new world speed record of over 140 m.p.h. The design included filling the light hull with ping-pong balls to provide air pockets to prevent the boat from sinking in case it was holed. We thought it was a great idea, and we were sure Sir Malcolm wouldn't mind if we adapted it.

Do you know how many ping-pong balls it would take to fill the hull of a canoe? More than our pocket money would buy! Undaunted, Beezer came up with a solution. We would simply collect empty tin cans with the lids partially attached and seal them with chewing gum to keep the air in and the water out. Then we would fill the bottom of the hull with these miniature buoyancy tanks.

Soon it was time for the test launch. The canoe turned out to be surprisingly heavy to carry. To solve the problem we got out my wooden wagon, tied the canoe on top of it and pulled it up to Nigel Cummings' house. Nigel was enthusiastic about helping us launch it on his pond. We didn't have a bottle of champagne for a proper launch so we used some fizzy pop, tying the bottle to a piece of string and swinging it against the bow of the canoe, chanting *"El Verde Diablo Pequeño!"* Unfortunately, the bottle didn't break, and our attempt at a christening ended with nothing to show for it but a dent in the canoe's bow, easy enough to touch up with a dab of paint scraped from the bottom of the nearly empty can.

We went ahead with the launching while resuming our chanting. Unfortunately the canoe dived bow first under the surface of the pond, became water logged, and sank. Our hearts sank with it, and we got muddy climbing into the pond in a struggle to pull it out. All we had accomplished was to frighten the goldfish! The sinking probably happened because we got the angle of launch too steep, and also the hull got tangled up in the water lilies. That wouldn't be a problem when we got to the River Fowey. We trucked the canoe home and touched up some of the gaps in the fabric with more paint.

We looked forward to the camping trip, and now the time was upon us. The Pathfinders piled tents, sleeping bags, cooking equipment, and kit bags into a couple of vans, and we hoisted our canoe on top. Off we all headed to the farm by the river, singing campfire songs and in a jolly good mood. As soon as we arrived we pitched our tents in orderly lines, dug latrines, and set up our cooking area. By the time we finished it was dark and time for "lights out", so the launch would have to wait until the next day.

I brought my trumpet with me, and I woke up early the next morning and sounded the Reveille. Everyone got up, cooked, and ate breakfast as quickly as possible so we could set off for the river bank. Beezer and I were glad of some help carrying our canoe over the field to the launch site.

El Verde Diablo Pequeño looked magnificent in her green livery. The Pathfinders clapped and cheered when we launched her. I was smaller than Beezer, so I got in first with my paddle while he held her by the stern in the shallows. Then with a great shove he pushed her out into the deeper current. What a moment of excitement!

The excitement soon turned into another heart-sinking disappointment. Before I could paddle more than three strokes, she sank like a stone. I was glad I had worn a bathing suit, as I was soaked. We tried to lift her out, so we could work on a redesign and try again, but she was full of water and so heavy that we couldn't possibly lift her off the bottom. In the end we had to abandon her and leave her to break up and rot in the fast running river.

The only boating we did that trip was in a hired rowboat with a professional oarsman. We couldn't bring ourselves to enjoy it much. The rest of the time we practiced our knots, did gymnastics, played games and went on exploring expeditions. Our camping trip was over too soon, and we took down our tents, packed up our equipment, filled in the latrines, and headed home in the vans. Alas, no canoe.

When we got home, Beezer and I went to collect more engine numbers and fill out the County class, but we got bored after a while. Moving on to another project, we decided to either build a telescope and do some serious astronomy or maybe start a new political party. Before we got to either one, the war ended and the evacuee program ended too. There was nothing we could do about that. Beezer had to return to London right away to rejoin his family. It was sadder losing my best friend than losing our canoe.

Fag!

At age thirteen or so my parents sent me away to school. I had been perfectly happy at the grammar school in my childhood Cornish town, but my parents had high expectations of their children educationally. They became comfortably off as my father's career progressed, but were not wealthy and had to choose where they spent their money. Like most of their neighbors they regarded owning a car as a nonessential luxury, and if truth be told, an impenetrable mechanical mystery. Their priority was our education.

Both my elder sisters did well at school: head girls, one a captain of sports teams, the other a star in the school play. Pam became the first girl from Cornwall to go up to Cambridge where she read English and later economics. Pat studied at the Bristol Royal Infirmary and qualified as a physiotherapist.

My parents' choice of school for me was Clifton College. It was aiming high given that I had not gone to a private preparatory school, but my father felt he might as well stretch his financial commitment to go first class. In the final analysis, my mother's whim of iron decided on what was best for her children. Also my cousin, whose father was the steward for Viscount Clifden managing the great Lanhydrock estate, had gone there to School House, which provided a connection. Clifton was a Westcountry school, relocated to its home on the Bristol Downs at the edge of the city after being evacuated to a Cornish seaside town during the war. Further, it was comfortably Anglican, less military than Wellington, less athletic than Sherborne, and less terrifyingly academic than Winchester.

I had to pass the common entrance examination in order to get in. This was a challenge. Latin was the major requirement. The Liskeard Grammar School offered a choice between Latin and biology after the second form. Since at the time I was set on a career as a kindly rural veterinary surgeon, I chose biology, although how I would ever deal later with the Latin requirement to enter university was not pointed out to me. Fortunately, there was a retired missionary in Liskeard who agreed to coach me. So when I went up to Clifton to sit the entrance exam I was modestly confident that I might eke out a scholarship to help with the fees.

The other candidates proved awesome. I was literally out of their class. They had all studied Latin since they first went to boarding school at the age of seven, and many of them classical Greek, too. Their mathematics were advanced, their French Parisian, their English impeccable. I could not even correctly pronounce the surname of the winner of the major scholarship, Marjoribanks (spoken as "*Marchbanks*").

I was advised to stick to elementary mathematics for the second examination paper in that subject after my shortcomings were revealed by my answers to the first one. I am sure I was better than the other boys at biology and physics, but these were not deemed worthy of examination.

Interviews went well, particularly with the housemaster of School House, Martin Hardcastle. I apparently did well enough to get a place and win a minor scholarship, an "exhibition" as it was termed. To give me an extra year to prepare for the school leaving certificate and university entrance, I was told to repeat the fourth form and was demoted from the A to the B stream until I improved my Latin. Apparently my modest success was based more on promise than accomplishment.

The summer of 1945 was eventful. In June the war ended. Then in July the Labour party resoundingly beat Churchill in the general election, and the Conservatives and the Liberals were trounced. By September, my life at Clifton started with a tea in School House for new boys and their families on the first day of term. It was a stilted affair, since few of us knew each other, but it got us introduced. The housemaster, Mr. Hardcastle, hosted the tea. He was a bachelor, so the house matron, Miss Andrews, acted as hostess, and they were supported by the house tutor, the Reverend J.M. Grove, widely known as Olly. As well as assisting in running the house, Olly was one of the school's two Anglican chaplains and also taught classics. The three of them lived in the house on the private side.

Boarding school life was full and very different from the way I had grown up. I was too busy to be homesick. There was so much to learn, not just school lessons but traditions, customs, privileges, slang, names, games, timetables, places, where to go, how to get around, what to avoid, and rules and punishments.

I did write the obligatory letter home every Sunday, enquiring after the wellbeing of my amazing cat Tigger and my racing pigeons, and looking forward to my parents visit at half term. I welcomed my father's barely legible notes of encouragement, my mother's elegantly calligraphed letters of news from home and concerns about whether my bed was properly aired, and my sisters' occasional shafts of humor. Letters were our only communication. There was no telephone for us boys, although we could use the housemaster's in the rare event of emergency. Long distance calls were an extravagance.

My big sister Pat was kind enough in her time off from her job at the Bristol Royal Infirmary to come and see me at school and make sure that I suffered no vestiges of home sickness. She made a point of taking me out to tea. There was a chain of excellent teashops in the city with the inspired slogan, "There is only one T in Bristol, Carwardines". We would catch a bus to Blackboy Hill (shades of the slave trade!) to Carwardines where she would teach me the etiquette of escorting a lady out to tea.

She would instruct me on helping her off with her coat and holding her chair for her while she sat at the table. She ensured that the waitress gave me the menu, which I first showed to Pat before making my own choice. I would invite her to pour, since that was the lady's role. I had to ask the waitress to bring me the bill since I was the gentleman, but fortunately Pat surreptitiously gave me the money to pay and guided me on the correct amount of the tip.

Back at school I learned many other lessons of value in later life. Academics, sports, and music were excellent at Clifton. The strong military tradition had the O.T.C. (Officers Training Corps) parading every Monday on the quadrangle in front of the statue of Field Marshall Earl Haig, an Old Cliftonian and commander-in-chief of the British Army on the western front in the Great War. We were put through drill maneuvers and taught the operation and care of the Lee-

Enfield rifle and the Bren gun. The elements of command were thoroughly instilled in us.

The school provided a wide range of activities. My favorite was the scientific society with field trips including visits to a brewery, a cider works and a cigarette factory. One old hand pronounced that the school had an unspoken code that ensured that every boy could do well at something, with plenty of competition to keep us focused. That way most were satisfied with their lot, and there were few troublemakers. He said we were all classified either as "hearties", "arties" or "smarties".

The school had an ingenious way of dealing with the older hearties, the athletic types who lacked the brains to shine in the classroom or the character to be given responsibility. They were officially appointed to a shadowy institution known as Big Side Levée, which was nominally consulted on matters of sports but in practice had no power or influence and never met.

Big Side was on the Close, the field at the heart of the school grounds where the first Rugby XV and cricket XI played their matches with visiting schools, watched by the whole school. Team sports, including field hockey, rowing, shooting and athletics, were important, as well as individual games of tennis, rackets, squash, fives, boxing and cross-country running. There were practices or matches every afternoon except Sunday and Monday. No doubt rigorous exercise was good for the moral development of pubescent boys.

As well as the school teams, every house had teams for all age groups, culminating at the end of term with knock-out tournaments vying to be champion, or "Cock House". School House was short on individual stars, but we prided ourselves on winning through the house spirit inculcated by our beloved housemaster "Cassy", as Mr. Hardcastle was known fondly if not very imaginatively.

The intense competition between the houses extended to music and art contests. School House lacked music scholars, so rather than soloists our tradition was to enter an orchestra. It was a motley ensemble made up of whatever instrument we could muster, including violins, a tuba, a clarinet, a trombone and my trumpet. The judges always commended our enthusiasm. Music was important at Clifton with a high standard ensured by music scholarships, a professionally staffed music school, and performances by a military band, a symphony orchestra, a choral society and a chapel choir, sometimes at outside venues like Bristol Cathedral.

The school was organized as a sort of federal system. The board of governors set broad policy and guided finances. The headmaster led the school's staff, assisted by heads of departments looking after education and academic standards, with housemasters guiding the personal lives of the boys. The head of each house and a few other senior boys were appointed "praeposters" (as prefects were called) to take leadership in school activities and societies and the O.T.C. The head of the school had the privilege of wearing a moustache and getting married, although neither of these had been exercised in living memory. Praeposters had authority to discipline any boy. It took a serious offense for a master to get involved or for severe discipline to be applied in the case of academic shortcomings. In the rare event of an extremely serious offense like stealing, the headmaster would step in and it could result in expulsion.

We were assigned to forms according to our ability at Latin, which we studied with our form master, as well as English and Old and New Testaments. We were assigned seats in the order in which we had ranked in the end of term exams, with boys at the bottom seated in the front. For other subjects we were placed in sets according to our shortcomings or special talents. I particularly enjoyed physics and chemistry in the well-equipped modern science school.

Since the war and ongoing rationing, meals were no longer prepared and served in the individual houses but in Big School, with all 500 boys eating together with a sprinkling of masters. It was partly about efficiency and economy of scale (particularly in the case of whale meat that was tough yet officially nutritious) and also a desire to ease the segregation of houses, although we were still assigned places at table by rank in houses. At lunch and dinner the headmaster presided at high table and said grace in Latin, with proper attention to the tense of the verb depending on whether the grace preceded or followed the meal.

Every morning after breakfast we went to Chapel, passing the inspection of the school Marshall (a retired army sergeant-major) who made sure our shoes were polished, involving buffing on the backs of our trouser legs to get by. We took our assigned seats for a compulsory service conducted by the school's Anglican chaplains. Every Sunday there was an optional early communion for those who were confirmed Anglicans and a compulsory morning service and sung Evensong twice a term. Sometimes there would be a visiting bishop or canon, and once a term the headmaster would preach a scholarly and uplifting sermon. Jewish boys attended synagogue in their own house, Polack's.

Our lives outside the classroom centered on the house. There were six for boarders and two for day boys, each with distinctive personalities and traditions. Upon arrival at School House we were assigned small rooms, "studies", where we kept our personal belongings and books with a desk on which to do extra classwork. Studies were for two or three junior boys or one senior boy, providing a modicum of privacy during the day. The senior boy was called a "house sixth", and his study was at the entrance to each corridor of studies.

We were also assigned study mates, whom we could exchange for someone of our own choice after the first term. My study mate was R.N.D Kidd, minor. He had an elder brother in the house, Kidd major. They had grown up in Ireland where their grandfather was the vicar of Downpatrick. We all called each other by our surnames, hardly knew each other's Christian names. Kidd and I proved compatible, became good friends, visited each other's homes during the holidays, and remained study mates until he left Clifton.

House sixths were in charge of routine discipline within the boarding houses and were empowered to impose punishments up to and including beating. There were lots of rules. Breaking them, such as running or fighting in the corridor, disobeying or being impertinent to a house sixth (being "gassy"); siding (which was leaving your jacket unbuttoned or putting your hands in your trouser pockets); and talking after lights out were all punishable by "lines".

Minor offences were punished by 50 or 100 lines, not in those enlightened times in the form of repetitively writing a rote promise to reform but rather by memorizing a Shakespeare sonnet or a Horace ode. However, if you accumulated 500 lines within one term you got a house beating; four strokes on your buttocks for a first offence, six or eight if you were incorrigible. These were ritualistic affairs, administered in your pyjamas after lights-out by the head of the house and his lieutenant. We innocents lay in our beds in the dark counting the cracks and then silently welcoming the stiff-upper-lipped new hero back to his bed.

House sixths had responsibilities but also enjoyed privileges, such as a solo study at the end of each corridor. At night the sixth had the bed at the end of the dormitory and could stay up after lights out. He was allowed to "side", and was a member of the house Anchor Club with its own common room. Above all, they had "fags". New boys were fags for their first two or three terms until they were promoted to non-fag or little fifth. If the sixth wanted something done, for example, his shoes polished, his study tidied, his brass corps cap badge and belt buckles polished, his gaiters Blancoed (Blanco was a special product that came in green for military webbing or white for cricket boots or pads), he would go out of his study and shout "Faaag!" The fags would hare out of their studies down to the end of the corridor and the last one would get the job.

The head of the house chose three personal fags from the more senior ones, each taking turns to fag for him one week at a time. I fagged for R.T.M. Lindsay, which was quite a privilege because he was also head of the school, corps commander, captain of cricket and Rugby football. For school cricket matches my most important jobs were oiling his cricket bat and Blancoing his white wicket-keeper's pads to cover the grass stains.

We slept in communal dormitories assigned by seniority, each one under the supervision of a house sixth. Lockers and hanging spaces were assigned for clothes. I enquired about the floor to ceiling steel barred gates sealing off the stairs leading to the dormitory on the third floor. Apparently they had been installed to restore order after the "fags' rebellion" in the nineteenth century but had not been locked in recent years. Good grief, Clifton was going to take some getting used to!

Our days started with a bell at ten past seven. The seventeen boys in my dormitory (excluding the house sixth who was in charge and excused such rules) leapt out of our iron beds and into dressing gowns and slippers and rushed down to the communal "pan rooms" in the basement, one for senior and one for junior boys.

The plumbing was luxurious by English standards since it had been remodeled by General Omar Bradley and his American staff when they were billeted in School House while planning D-Day. We had twenty minutes to get back upstairs and dressed and back down to the house hall on the ground floor for "call-over".

The house sixth in charge would call out "Two" at 7.28 a.m., "One" at 7:29 a.m. and "J.I.T." (Just in Time) on the dot of half past, at which point he would slam the door shut, bar further admission, and conduct "call-over". If you were not there to answer when your name was called, you got a "late". If you accumulated four lates in the course of a term you got a house beating. Most boys tried to be in time, thus learning the virtue of punctuality.

After call-over we went back to our dormitories and made our beds, tidied up and got properly dressed. We wore uniforms: plain grey suit with long trousers, grey socks, black laced shoes, white shirt with optional thin black stripes, and a detachable white soft collar that required a front and back stud, and a plain navy blue tie. In the summer term we could wear a cooler unlined grey blazer with navy blue piping.

We wore distinctive small black caps that sat precariously on the back of one's head. Ribbons sewn on the caps formed stripes, and the color identified your house. The School House color was a reddish orange. You had to wear your cap when you were off the school premises or out of doors on the school grounds, except when playing games, except for cricket when one wore a cricket cap, except when you were bowling when the umpire held your cap for you. Except, since School House was the first house when the school was founded, we enjoyed the privilege of not wearing our caps on the school grounds.

We had great pride in School House. Martin Hardcastle was unchallengeably the best housemaster in the school; we respected him and loved him. He taught us, like William of Wykeham, that "Manners Makyth Man". Never give in to alarm and despondency. He suggested rather than directed. He did not actually *say* never boast, never bully, that truthfulness, honour, duty, integrity and loyalty were fundamental values; these virtues were simply without question, imbued in the spirit of his house. He made us special, indeed unique. He was progressive, and during our time he liberalized some of the more hidebound customs.

We did things no other house did. We competed successfully as teams, without stars. We ended each term with a house entertainment, featuring the Gilbert & Sullivan songs he taught us, the sketches and parodies we wrote and performed, rollicking fun with the female impersonation so beloved of English music hall.

We had Anchor Nights (the private term we used was "arries") on the Clifton Downs on a Saturday night when Cassy created elaborate plots with the fags capturing and beating up house sixths disguised as dangerous foreign spies. We had a first-class croquet court on the lawn.

Cassy took us climbing and caving. One night he woke four of us at midnight and took us out to climb Cheddar Gorge with ropes in the moonlight, followed by skinny dipping in the school swimming pool. Cassy arranged for the senior boys to have dancing lessons with the neighboring girls school.

At Christmas we had a dance in the house hall where we could invite our girlfriends. That is where I met my first wife, the prettiest girl at the neighboring Clifton High School for Girls, and also my lifelong chum, the irrepressible Shirley, who later preferred to be known as Clare.

Other masters contributed to our experiences of life beyond the school bounds. Dr. Fox, the eccentric director of music, took a few of us to a gala performance at Bristol's Colston Hall. This magnificent building was bombed during the war, and the special event was to celebrate its reconstruction and reopening. The famed London Philharmonic Orchestra, under its dynamic conductor Sir Thomas Beecham, performed with the Bristol Choral Society. There was a festive banquet afterwards at which the new lord mayor spoke. He was the city's first Socialist lord mayor and a fine public servant, but lacking the social polish of his predecessors. His speech was unconventional. "I'd like to thank Tom Beecham and his band," he rumbled. "There's nothin' like a good old sing-song to warm the cockles of yer 'eart!"

A few years ago, some twenty or so of us arranged an unofficial reunion, climaxed with a banquet at the Bristol Merchant Venturers Hall. We were drawn together by lifetime friendships and our loving memories of our housemaster. The old house had changed since our day but certainly was not improved by what our successors saw as progress. Why, they allow girls in the school nowadays. Nobody said it, but the looks in our eyes told us that our schooldays were some of the happiest days of our lives.

What a strange experience it must seem to those who hear of life at Clifton but did not live it. What was the point of the odd traditions, the regimentation, the hierarchies, the pettifogging rules, the code of privilege and punishment? We certainly enjoyed a magnificent education enriching our lives to an extraordinary degree. But beyond the scholars and the academics and the scientists, the great public schools set out to train leaders, rulers of empire, explorers, statesmen, military officers, public servants, business executives, entertainers, sportsmen, and community leaders.

Before we became leaders we were taught to become followers and to serve. When we became leaders we had already learned to exercise authority with responsibility.

We were imbued with a sense of belonging to something special, of having a duty to contribute to our world, and to set an example. In the words of the Old Cliftonian poet, Sir Henry Newbolt, we were taught, "To set the cause above renown, to love the game beyond the prize."

It is all so quaint, so old-fashioned. I cherish the tradition.

Breakthrough

I told my father I wanted to go into the family business as soon as possible after I left school, once I got National Service out of the way. What was the point of going to the university? I had all the general education that was necessary. What I needed next were the technical knowledge and skills required to run a newspaper and printing business.

As for the National Service, I was not keen on going into my father's old regiment, the Duke of Cornwall's Light Infantry. The infantry fought hand to hand with bayonets and went on long route marches, in the case of the D.C.L.I. at an exhaustingly fast pace. I researched the possibilities and fancied something safer and less athletic, something far behind the front line such as the Royal Artillery, or better still something sedentary and not involved in fighting at all such as the Intelligence Corps.

However, that decision proved unnecessary. The government decided that things had settled down enough after the war to reduce National Service from two years to eighteen months and to make it more selective. When I went for the army medical examination, the doctors were concerned about my occasional heart palpitations. They had started when I was about fourteen and had their uses, such as excusing me from boxing and physical training. I was still allowed to play the games I enjoyed, rugger, field hockey, tennis and chess. The medical board had me examined by a psychologist (a novel experience) to make sure I was not malingering. It then concluded that I was a risk for a disability pension resulting from the stress of military exertions and refused to pass me, with a caution that with care I might survive to middle age.

My father stepped in with what in retrospect was sound advice but that at the time I was too impatient to accept with good grace. Now, I have long given up the foolish fantasy that my grandchildren might read my memoirs, but I must for the record make a statement that they may find incredible if not heretical.

Parents are sometimes right.

My father said, "Have two strings to your bow, my son." He thought that a university education and degree would give me the option for an alternative career. All very well, Dad, but what could possibly go wrong? Being habitually obedient I decided to follow in my sister's footsteps and go to Cambridge. I researched the colleges to decide on my favorites, awarding them points for fundamental factors such as their propinquity to the River Cam and convenience for punting: being on "the backs" as it was called.

However, as so often happens, my best laid plans "ganged agley". My history master said that Clifton had a closed scholarship with The Queen's College, Oxford, and I might have a chance of winning an award. My results in history in the advanced examinations, set by the government Ministry of Education to certify fitness for leaving school, were good enough that I could get a generous state scholarship so there would be little financial burden on my family. Furthermore, the Oxford exams were earlier than those at Cambridge so I could practice on Oxford and go on to Cambridge anyway.

A handful of us took the train from Bristol to Oxford for a few days to sit the exams. I shared a room with Dan Hooper. Dan was an eccentric, not a scholar. However, our headmaster, Sir Desmond Lee, a distinguished academic and former Cambridge don, persuaded the fellows of Queen's that Hooper would add leaven to college life and he was admitted.

We should have done last minute swotting, but instead Dan and I spent the evenings celebrating our newfound independence from school restrictions by drinking cheap wine from the tooth mugs in our room. Dan regaled me with stories of school holidays spent in his uncle's sea-side cottage in Spain skinny dipping in the moonlight with their maid and rolling around on the sand clothed only in seaweed. Enterprising fellow that he was, he later parleyed that cottage into a chain to make a fortune in a company called "Rent-a-Villa." He was named the "Entrepreneur of the Year" in a business magazine and later became more famous when he was imprisoned for defrauding investors.

As things turned out, I won a place at Oxford and was awarded an exhibition (a minor scholarship); quite a breakthrough.

Academically, I decided to stay with my specialty at school and study history, a good background for my chosen career in journalism. In our first two terms we had to get through four preliminary exams: historical geography, Bede's *History of the English Church* in the Latin, political theory (based on Aristotle, Hobbes, Locke and Rousseau) and Latin translation. After that we prepared for final examinations at the end of the third year.

This entailed writing two essays each week. We read these to our tutors during the tutorial, usually shared with one other undergraduate. Preparation typically involved reading two or three books and half a dozen articles for each and arguing for competing interpretations. The university provided lectures. It was a joy to attend those by famous and entertaining professors such as A.J.P. Taylor, Hugh Trevor-Roper and Cecil Day-Lewis, who later was appointed poet laureate. Lectures were not necessarily coordinated with the topics we were studying with our tutors, so we kept notes that we could refer to at appropriate times.

Studies took up a great deal of our time, and to make time for exercise and social life we would often write our essays during the night before our tutorials. I had rowed briefly in fours at Clifton but did not take up eights at Oxford; rowing was extremely time consuming. I played squash enthusiastically and hockey poorly. I played rugger once and was completely outclassed. I patronized the cozy pubs and their endless conversation, especially the Queen's favorite Eastgate Tavern and The Bear, tucked behind The High since 1242 and now with a huge collection of school, club and regimental ties displayed on the walls.

I took afternoon tea at the fashionable restaurants with old school friends where people went to be seen by the beautiful people. One friend, an Old Cliftonian, was one of the few undergraduates with a car, a Sunbeam-Talbot coupé. He had to get permission from the proctors and display a green light on the front bumper. We would drive out into the Cotswolds and eat splendid food at The Bear in Woodstock (with Blenheim Palace just around the corner) or The Lamb at Burford. These were a welcome change from dinners in the college hall which were passably good but limited by the wartime rationing that still persisted.

Breakthrough ❧ ❧ page 58

There were lots of parties. Mine in my second year became famous. I have told the story before, but it is worth repeating here. My room on the back quad across from the library was spacious. We crammed more than fifty people into it: politicians, actors, poets, socialites, athletes, aesthetes, old school friends and, fortunately, my neighbor across the hall, the dean who was in charge of college discipline, Charlie Kennedy. The drinks were economical but lethal: "Tanglefoot" (a mix of gin and hard cider) and a wine punch whose kick was disguised by the addition of lichée juice. My scout kept the drinks flowing as fast as the conversation.

The food was a spectacular treat, provided by my girlfriend, a splendid Cordon Bleu trained chef who later became my wife. She tastefully arranged all the food (canapés, watercress sandwiches, cheese straws, brandy snaps, tartlets, miniature éclairs) on a table in the middle of the room. Upon the unveiling all the guests, including the dean, crowded hungrily around the table at the same time.

There was a resounding crack. The floor sagged several inches. We had broken a three hundred-year-old, two-foot-square oak floor joist. The crowd fled through the door without saying thank-you or goodbye. Fortunately nobody was hurt, and more fortunately I heard nothing from college authorities. They installed a temporary pillar to support the floor in the room below, which was occupied by a Canadian Rhodes scholar who was welcoming his girlfriend before coming up to join us. Apparently her enthusiasm was dampened. He later dealt with the situation by decorating the pillar as a totem pole and installing a beer keg against it with a tap that some imbibers interpreted as a fertility symbol.

The floor was quietly repaired during the next vacation, and I heard no more about the incident until a couple of years later. My brother-in-law had a school friend who went up to Queen's. He announced with pride that he had been assigned the room in which the famous party was held where they broke the floor.

I became deeply involved in politics. I joined the Union, ate in its dining room, used its library, attended its parliamentary style debates, and occasionally spoke, once as a featured "paper" speaker, and ran narrowly unsuccessfully for election to a committee. I became active in the Liberal Club, eventually being elected president. My counterparts in the conservative Blue Ribbon Club were Michael Heseltine (he later became an M.P. and deputy leader of the Conservative Party in the House of Commons and a peer) and in the socialist Labour Club Anthony Howard (who became American correspondent and later editor of The Economist).

My predecessor as president of the Liberal Club was Jeremy Thorpe, handsome, flamboyant, dashing, ambitious, president of the Union, a product of Eton and Trinity, an urbane man-about-town recognized for his elegant tailored suits and brown bowler hat. He founded the Russell and Palmerston Club for former officers of the O.U. Liberal Club. At our meetings to discuss affairs of state we toasted, "The Lords Russell and Palmerston and the Party that they served."

He was elected Member of Parliament for a Westcountry constituency near Cornwall and became friends with our Liberal M.P., Peter Bessell (who had defeated Sir Douglas Marshall). Peter at one point was interested in buying *The Cornish Times* when my father retired. We were all fellow members of the National Liberal Club in London, near Old Scotland Yard. Jeremy arranged for the Liberal party's annual conference to be held in his constituency.

I led the Oxford delegation, and together with our Cambridge compatriots we created quite a stir, much to Jeremy's delight. My heroine Lady Violet Bonham-Carter (daughter of Liberal Prime Minister Herbert Asquith, friend of Winston Churchill) was a charming and forceful presence and I fondly remember her pleasure when I presented her on stage with a huge bouquet of Irises. When Jeremy starred at a Liberal rally at the Cornish home of the great Isaac Foot I was a supporting speaker. Jeremy went on to become the youngest leader of the parliamentary Liberal Party.

Later, their lives fell apart dramatically. Jeremy Thorpe was accused of arranging, with Peter Bessell's help, the attempted murder of his homosexual lover on Dartmoor. He was forced to resign as Liberal leader. After a sensational trial at the Old Bailey and a controversial summing up by the judge, Jeremy was acquitted. He left public life. Peter Bessell left England and fled to America where he failed in business after being accused of fraud. The story was made into a successful television series *A Very English Scandal*, with a convincing performance by Hugh Grant as Jeremy Thorpe. It was stunning to observe such sensational changes of fortune in the lives of people one once knew and admired.

Political life had its social side, too. We invited John Arlott to speak after dinner at our Liberal Club annual banquet. He was a well-known cricket commentator for the BBC with a laconic and dryly amusing style of commentary delivered with a Westcountry burr. He told a story about the famous England fast bowler, Freddy Truman. Freddy was a Yorkshireman with the sturdy physique of one who had grown up in the working class. He was noted for aggressive impatience more than diplomacy or social skills. The selectors for the English touring side had some doubts as to the wisdom of including him in the party that went to the West Indies but concluded that his athletic skills could not be spared. After all, the tour included gentlemen who could mentor him.

A cricket tour is part international competition and part unofficial state visit to various Commonwealth countries. A talented West Indian team soundly defeated the British cricketers, and after the match entertained their guests at a lavish state banquet. Freddy Truman was seated next to a leading politician from the native party, an influential leader important to impress. The gentleman fell asleep at his place soon after the entrée was served. Freddy did not take to being ignored. In one of those silences that falls on a gathering when one wishes it would not, Freddy nudged his neighbor sharply in the ribs and said in a loud Yorkshire accent, "Wake up, Gunga Din, and pass the bloody salt!"

Memories While Memory Lasts ❧ ❧ page 61

Brilliant Minds

These days my contemporaries are dying, in most cases moving on to their just rewards, whatever those might be. In August 2015 Dr. Oliver Sacks succumbed to cancer. He practiced and taught neurology, but his most acclaimed career was as a writer on neurological topics, telling engaging stories of his patients in a style that communicated medical arcana to a wide lay audience. I knew him as an undergraduate at Oxford, and his admirers have on occasion called me in to speak about what I know about this strange and gifted man, what light I might shed on his brilliance, and what motivated and formed him.

Indeed, Oliver Sacks is a vivid part of my memories of student days. I knew him as a neighbor and acquaintance in my social circle as well as through the impressions of his fellow students. We both came up in 1951 to The Queen's College, Oxford, Oliver to read medicine and me to read history. After intending to follow in my sister's footsteps to Cambridge I ended up at Oxford, because my school offered a closed scholarship that was exclusive to pupils of Clifton College and members of the Neale family. Clifton was known for having a Jewish boarding house and for welcoming American students, both of which groups were among my friends at the university.

One such Old Cliftonian friend was Michael Tarsh whose family were prominent members of the Jewish community in Liverpool and exemplified their culture's aspiration to distinguished professional careers. His mother was a barrister, exceptional for a woman in those days, and his father was a physician who changed careers in mid-life to become a barrister also. Michael read medicine, and his friends became part of my circle. Michael was the only medical student I knew who was unabashedly in it for the money.

The Tarsh and Sacks families knew each other well, and Michael spoke glowingly of the brilliant scholar from a well-connected family who was coming up to Queen's and introduced us. Oliver Sacks was different. He tended to be reclusive and aloof. He participated little in college social life and not at all in team sports (he was not built for speed). He was rarely seen in the Junior Common Room. Perhaps his speaking voice inhibited him; he had something of a speech impediment, a lisp, and he wheezed. When he was not in the labs at the medical school he spent time in his room.

I am asked about what I know of Oliver's early life, so important to understanding a person's psychological makeup. However, in the fifties in Britain there was limited awareness of psychiatry or psychotherapy, and my contemporaries were not deeply curious about each other's emotional history, even among close friends. We did not talk about trauma or depression; the cure for suffering or feeling down was to brace up and keep a stiff upper lip.

So what I know of Oliver's youth I learned from his autobiography *On the Move*, published near the time of his death. We, of course, were the generation whose early lives were formed during World War II with its terrors and disruptions. Like so many Londoners, Oliver Sacks and his brother Michael were evacuated to escape the blitz. Evacuation was a huge upheaval; altogether there were some 1.5 million evacuees, about half of them children. Thousands more went to America and to further reaches of the British Empire. The Sacks brothers were sent to board at a preparatory school (in the English sense of private pre-secondary) in the Midlands for eighteen months. Oliver does not describe where they spent the school holidays, although it's likely they stayed with a local family.

In remote, rural, non-strategic Cornwall where I grew up, we welcomed evacuees from the big cities into our homes. They arrived by train in forlorn groups carrying their suitcases with their gas masks slung over their shoulders, homesick and missing their families, but we soon cheered them up.

Oliver and his brother had a much worse experience. In *On The Move* Oliver describes the headmaster of the school, Braefield, as a sadist who delighted in beating his pupils. He went on to say that Michael was sent on to public school at Clifton where "he was unmercifully bullied". His back was "full of weals and bruises". Michael became severely mentally disturbed and was finally diagnosed with schizophrenia. Oliver suggests this was attributable, at least in part, to the bullying at Clifton.

I have to say that Michael Sacks was in Polack's House, the boarding house exclusively for Jewish boys. It was led by four generations of the Polack family, fine men and great educators. I may be idealizing my schooldays, but I find it hard to accept that serious bullying would have been unobserved, let alone condoned, by any of the masters or praeposters (senior boys) in Polack's. Beating was still the punishment of last resort at Clifton but it was infrequent and carefully controlled.

Incidentally, after bombs struck its buildings the entire school was evacuated from the strategic port city of Bristol to a quiet resort town in Cornwall.

At Oxford Oliver and I were close, if not intimate, during our second year. We had rooms on the same staircase in the back quad, Oliver at the front on the ground floor (it had to bear the weight of his grand piano) and me in the room above.

Some half a dozen of us, medical students, philosophers, historians, classicists, economists, politicians and musicians, would regularly meet in one of our rooms on our staircase (never Oliver's) for late night drinks and conversation. Oliver came out of hiding for these gatherings, and his intelligence and the catholic breadth of his reading showed up during our discussions. Other qualities showed up too. His intellectual arrogance was unapologetically clear, and he was careful to limit his participation to those topics where he could shine. In his contributions there was a trace of cruelty. He regaled us with a shocking story of his relationship with a rather dowdy undergraduate at St. Hilda's, also Jewish. He encouraged her to fall in love with him and then dumped her. He explained this as an experiment he conducted to observe her resulting emotional state.

During that year Oliver's cousin Anna Landau (Landau was his mother's maiden name) came up to St. Hilda's with fanfare similar to Oliver's. She was strikingly beautiful with rich red hair and a porcelain complexion, progressive politically. Eventually, she joined the Liberal Club of which I was president and became an active committee member. I was not aware of the cousins seeing much of each other.

We lived well. The scout for our staircase was Jim Lewendon, who cleaned our rooms, made our beds, and kept up our fires. Jim became a good friend and was the butler at my wedding reception. Years later his son Nigel became Steward, head of the college servants. When I took my second wife Penny to England it was Nigel who showed us over Queen's including parts I had never seen before, such as the vaults where our Charles I engraved silver beer tankards were stored. The college had by then followed the trend to co-education. Memorably, Nigel said, "Queen's has changed since your day, sir. The undergraduates walk around the quads holding hands. But they always did, didn't they sir?"

Anyway, I read Oliver's autobiography *On the Move* with interest and also the obituary published in the college *Record*. I learned much that I did not know about him, even during his Oxford days. However, some apparent lapses of memory on his part and differences in impression of events over sixty years ago caught my eye.

Oliver describes arriving from St. Paul's School in London to Oxford with a scholarship, taking the preliminary examinations for entry and failing them three times. Mr. Jones the Provost, who addressed him as "Sacks", told him that he had one more chance—which he took and succeeded in passing. That account does not add up. Customarily all senior members of the university addressed pupils as "Mister". Further, prelims are taken at the end of the first two terms. You may re-take a failed exam in the following term, but if you fail again you are rusticated, i.e. sent down to the country for a year to study harder and try one last time.

J.W. Jones, by the way, lacked the inspirational leadership of his predecessor, Oliver Franks. Lord Franks left Queen's when he was appointed British Ambassador to Washington. He later became Chairman of Lloyds Bank. Mr. Jones' notable accomplishment was an act of omission. He did not reopen the college brewery that was closed down during the war.

Oliver was fascinated by old books, their language as well as their content. The upper library at Queen's was the most magnificent room in Oxford, and I spent many happy hours in off-subject browsing of its priceless collections. That is where I learned that the cause of Henry VIII's obsession with Ann Boleyn was that she had three pairs of breasts. And there was an Elizabethan anatomy tome that used language much more colorful than today's modest Latin obscurity. The muscle known today as *levator externus ani* was to our forefathers with Anglo-Saxon robustness the *outside arse heaver*. There was another book that Oliver enthusiastically shared with his non-medical acquaintances, *Sexual Anomalies and Perversions* that I discreetly glimpsed.

Oliver describes Kalman Joseph Cohen as his best friend at Oxford. I did not realize that at the time or see them together. Kal and I met sitting next to each other on our first evening in Hall. The first course of our excellent dinner that night was honeydew melon, served in the English custom with powdered ginger. This was new to Kal, and with more enthusiasm than prudence he put a teaspoonful of ginger in his mouth to better taste it. Red-faced, spluttering and choking, Kal gulped down my water as well as his own. He was fortunate to escape being "sconced", the forfeit imposed for a breach of dining etiquette, consisting of drinking in one swallow the ceremonial two-pint tankard of college ale.

Kal was an American Rhodes scholar, a brilliant mathematician. He was researching an abstruse thesis in symbolic logic to take an M.Litt. in two years. He was advised against taking longer for a D.Phil. As he worked on his original theory, Einstein published a similar idea. This was a mere few weeks before Kal was to defend his thesis, and he had to scramble for a different original approach.

As Oliver describes, Kal was interested in girls, especially those who were physically well endowed, and avidly sought introductions. (Oliver writes extensively about his own homosexuality but few of us had any contemporary knowledge of this. It was a criminal offence at the time, and one did not blab it about.) Kal's most elegant introduction happened when I revived the custom of having dinner served in one's room. My girlfriend brought a college friend to meet Kal, but he found the setting with its handsome college china and silver and the exquisite cuisine served by my scout more to his taste than the determined virtue of our female guest.

On our first long vacation we hitchhiked across Europe together to a summer course in French language and culture at the University of Strasbourg where we joined fellow Queensmen. We stayed in

Youth Hostels but got few rides and finally had to resort to trains. Apparently Kal's appearance did us in. A kindly Belgian explained that bearded men wearing loud floral shirts were deemed either vagabonds or priests, and Kal did not appear to be a priest to him. By way of compensation we treated ourselves to *le bifstek et les pommes frites*, the first I had ever had.

Despite lack of multi-lingual conversational skills, Kal enjoyed an international array of girls from France, Spain, Denmark and Sweden. He apparently enjoyed the countryside too, exclaiming at intervals during our trip through the Vosges Mountains, "Gee, what a glorious panoramic vista!"

I left to go home. Kal continued on his travels. I learned from *On the Move* that Kal had then joined Oliver, traveling on to Germany. They stayed there with Gerhardt Sinsheimer from Queen's, a brilliant modern linguist, who unfortunately died young of a brain tumor. When we met back at Oxford I learned from Kal that his new buzz cut was due not to fashions in hairstyle but to an infestation of lice. After a distinguished academic career in the business school at Duke University, Kal died in 2010.

In his book Oliver also describes his dealings with Colin Haycraft, a successful publisher who worked to prepare Oliver's works for publication after difficulty in following the success of *Awakenings*. Colin was at Queen's too, a renaissance man. He was a classical scholar, won his half blue for squash, and was active in college affairs, a delightful and very accessible man. It seems a pity that Oliver missed the opportunity of meeting more of his fellow Queensmen, or they him.

During my third year I saw Oliver rarely after moving out of college into "digs" on St. John's Street (and never after going down from Oxford). My new neighbor on the ground floor was Andrew Johnson, a talented pianist and composer of cabaret songs for the Oxford Candlelight Club. They brought in talent from outside the university, including his girlfriend, an aspiring actress who had just left the local school to attend the new drama school at the Oxford Playhouse. She seemed shy for her chosen career but blossomed nevertheless. Her name was Maggie Smith. (I must say her roles were more prominent than my recorded trumpet fanfare on the battlements of Elsinore for an O.U. Dramatic Club production of *Hamlet.*)

Reading *On the Move* it seems that Oliver's widespread fame was more due to his wonderful writing than to his medical practice or research as a neurologist. He was also fortunate in his relatives and family connections in the world of writing and film-making. In articles in high quality lay publications, such as the *New York Review of Books* and the *New Yorker,* he polished the art of making accessible to the layman fascinating stories of odd neurological cases, illuminated with his extensive readings from bygone experts. These articles were collected into books that became best sellers around the world.

His fame really took off after the filming of *Awakenings* in 1990 with Robin Williams and Robert de Niro. The honors followed prolifically: awards, academy appointments, and fellowships, most noticeably an honorary fellowship at Queen's in 1999.

Queen's since its founding in 1341 has elected to fellowships many distinguished former members with lives of high achievement. In the same year as Oliver, Sir Tim Berners-Lee was elected for his development of the World-Wide Web while he was at CERN. Other fellows include Henry V of Plantagenet (king and musician), John Wycliffe (theologian who wrote the first English translation of the bible, a template for the St. James version), Joseph Addison (*The Spectator*), Edmund Halley (astronomer), Jeremy Bentham (philosopher), Edwin Hubble (astronomer), John Percival (first headmaster of Clifton College and Bishop of Hereford), Leopold Stokowski (conductor), Oliver Franks (Provost of Queen's, Ambassador to Washington, Chairman of Lloyds Bank), Ralph Vaughan Williams (composer), Rowan Atkinson (actor, script writer, creator of *Mr. Bean*), and Corey Booker (U.S. senator).

There were many stimulating members of the Junior Common Room. Andrew Hacker (whose Wikipedia biographer lists him as a "public intellectual") was a lively American political theorist whose recent article in the *New York Review of Books* appeared alongside Oliver's last contribution. Gerald Kaufman became a Labour M.P and government Secretary for Air, a persuasive debater and a kind encourager of aspiring Liberal politicians. After taking a first in law, Brian Simson was awarded a fellowship in All Souls, the college with only senior members devoted to research. Terry Granger was imprisoned in South Africa for his journalistic battle against apartheid. And even Old Cliftonian Dan Hooper had his day as "Entrepreneur of the Year" before he was arrested and imprisoned for fraud.

The products of universities like Oxford and colleges like Queen's contribute greatly to our civilization. Oliver Sacks was exceptional among them. He gave us stimulating stories of the mysterious workings of the human brain. Thank you, Oliver, for so expertly and elegantly opening this fascinating field of knowledge to us laymen. *Requiescat in pace.*

Eccentrics

Most young people find business a stark contrast to the life they enjoyed at their universities. However, from my experience in England, the worlds had much in common. I started my business life at Thomas Hedley & Co. Ltd., headquartered in the north of England in Newcastle upon Tyne and the British subsidiary of an American multi-national consumer goods company, the Procter and Gamble Company The work was absorbing, intellectually challenging, time consuming, competitive, and stressful. Above all, I was blessed with interesting colleagues from a similar background. There were four old members of my college in my marketing department alone, two linguists and two historians, all amiable gentlemen. A significant difference for most of us was that for the first time we had plenty of money in our pockets.

One of the linguists further enhanced his standard of living by marrying a brain surgeon. Soon after, he became impeccably dressed in bespoke suits, hand made by a tailor in London's famous Savile Row, long before the rest of us could afford such a display of luxury, indeed beyond many of our superiors too. We were not close friends, but as former members of the same college I felt I owed it to him to take the opportunity over a beer after work to mention tactfully that such display might be seen as inappropriate.

"You might consider, Dudley, old boy," I suggested, nervously using a mode of address that did not come naturally to me, "that in a hierarchical culture like this company, your splendid mode of dress might seem above your station. After all, there were some raised eyebrows when our young American contemporary could afford a far larger house than the rest of us."

Dudley pondered, but only briefly. "I've always wanted to be a snob. I'm not giving that up. The trouble is I have no social background, but at least I can look the part." Dudley seemed more troubled than I had realized.

My first boss Jack was from a working class family in Lancashire. He polished up his accent at Cambridge and went on to spend the war in the Intelligence Corps at the Pentagon monitoring radio signals from the Japanese navy. He was ingenious, original and brilliant. After starting a family and buying a house, he had little money left over for a car. Jack got a loan from his bank and bought a cheap old rattle-trap that did not run and that had a disintegrating interior. He did minimal work himself on the worst mechanical flaws so it at least operated. He reupholstered the body lining with a remnant of floral fabric. Jack proudly showed it off one evening when he drove me home after work. He took a strange roundabout route.

"Jack," I asked, "why are you going this way?"

"You'll see," he replied, concentrating on the turning ahead. After rounding a few more curves he drove up the hill below my house, changed gear to slow down and rubbed the tires against the curb by the entrance and coasted to a stop.

"I haven't fixed the brakes yet," he announced, smiling proudly. I never accepted a ride in that car again.

Jack's boss Gordon was at Cambridge with my brother-in-law, elegant, charming and articulate but with a stevedore's vocabulary. When he overheard his six year-old son Christopher swear at his mother he chastised him saying, "Holy shit, you rude little bugger! Where did you pick up that filthy bloody language?"

It was all so *English*, a phenomenon that at the time I had insufficient worldly experience to recognize, let alone cherish. Where else in the world could I have taken Rupert, my black Labrador retriever, to the office with me? (My wife and little daughter had gone to visit her parents for a few days so I was alone looking after our dog.) Rupert was well behaved and lay peacefully under my desk while I worked. When it was time for elevenses and the waitresses brought our coffee around, seeing Rupert stimulated a friendly pat on his head, a saucer of milk and a "Good boy!", nothing more. At lunchtime my calm and resourceful secretary Joan simply picked up his leash and took him for a walk through the grounds around the office building.

Rupert even received a friendly greeting by the dour Scot, Willie McCardy, whose intensity sharpened his intelligence to a needlepoint. Willie wore drip-dry shirts with a clip-on bow tie, sacrificing fashion on the altar of efficiency. He tried in vain to save the career of Malcolm Murphy-Bowen, whose gravitas was swamped by his irrepressible humor.

At the big meeting when the entire advertising agency team presented the storyboards for the crucial new TV campaign, the advertising director turned to Willie who turned to the brand manager who turned to Malcolm who leaned his elbows on the conference table, his chin in his hands, pondering interminably, seeking the profound strategic comment. Finally he looked up and asked, "Why does the man in the last picture have a bow tie, and the same man in the first picture have a straight tie?"

Malcolm unofficially rewrote the procedure book to the delight of his chums and the horror of his superiors with definitions like, "Suspense File: never put off until tomorrow what you can put off until the day after."

One Friday at lunch in the company dining room Malcolm ordered fish and chips. When the waitress presented it to him he peered at the plate and said, "Piece of Cod that passeth all understanding."

Malcolm was irrepressible. The inevitable day came when he was called into the closed-door one-on-one meeting in Willie's office. He was in there a long time. Malcolm eventually came out pale and shaken, saying, "I've just had my brain washed and I can't do a thing with it."

Working with the company's advertising agencies was a major and enjoyable part of our jobs. They were all based in London and most were American owned. They regarded entertaining the client as an essential business retention strategy, so we enjoyed perquisites including West End theatre, fine dining, and three martini lunches. From time to time, my counterpart at Young & Rubicam, Jack Casey, led his team's creative efforts in advertising our brand while enthusiastically prioritizing the entertaining aspect of his job, despite his advanced age. He must have been well into his fifties. He was also

American, so his rather strange mode of speech and behavior was a constant source of gentle amusement.

My personal highlight was when Jack took me to the varsity match at Twickenham when Oxford played Cambridge at Rugby football. Upon our arriving at the stadium in style in a chauffeur-driven Rolls Royce, Jack orchestrated the production from its luxurious boot (Jack called it a "trunk") of a picnic hamper equipped with fine china and crystal. Then the chauffeur served an elegant repast of cold roast chicken and asparagus accompanied by champagne.

We were in fine moods as we took our excellent seats to watch this ancient sporting rivalry at the home of English international Rugby football. After playing many first-class club sides, the varsity match was the climax of the university season for the keen rivals. The fifteen players on each team qualified to be awarded their "Blues", nicknamed after the colors of the dark blue shirts worn by Oxford and the light blue by Cambridge.

Jack's interest in the game was sparked by the presence of an unexpected member of the Oxford XV, an American football player with limited experience of the Rugby code. He was Pete Dawkins, now up at Brasenose College and a Rhodes scholar reading PPE (Politics, Philosophy and Economics). He was also a fine athlete and had won the American Heisman trophy after leading Army to an almost undefeated season while graduating first in his class at West Point.

The game was a defensive struggle. Disappointingly, Dawkins hardly touched the ball. Then Cambridge kicked the ball out of the field of play across the sideline, "out of touch". Play was restarted with a "line-out" with Dawkins throwing in the ball for Oxford. To the total surprise of the Cambridge forwards, Dawkins threw the ball quarterback style deep beyond the back of the line-out where it was caught by a speedy Oxford three-quarter back who started a breakaway. Jack could hardly contain his excitement. He leapt to his feet and bellowed, "Go Pete, go!"

A bowler-hatted elderly gentleman seated behind us wearing a Cambridge scarf was indignant at this untoward show of emotion. He tapped Jack on the shoulder with his rolled umbrella and spluttered,

"Young man, would you be kind enough to sit down and shut up and allow the rest of us to enjoy the game?"

And then there was Brian Barker. He was different. His genes came straight down from Ichabod Crane. He was shortsighted, tall, lanky, awkward, tight with money, an excellent modern linguist, and embarrassingly unpolished. Surprisingly, he was a first-class sportsman and played for the top teams of leading clubs. His batting on the cricket pitch was all elbows and lacked the style and grace admired by fans, but he successfully persisted in defending his wicket. On the Rugby field he played reliably in the critical position of full back, the last line of defense. He scrambled to the right place at the last minute, caught every ball cleanly, kicked with accuracy, and rarely let attackers get past him.

At the office Brian compensated for his shortcomings with hard work and amazing powers of concentration, an effective staff manager behind the scenes. Yet he was ambitious and successfully lobbied to be transferred to a line position. One day he was bent over his desk concentrating on his papers, writing feverishly. I heard his brand manager call over to him for a discussion.

"Brian, let's talk." Brian ignored the call and kept on writing. Annoyed, his manager yelled, "Brian, BRIAN!" until he finally got his attention.

Soon after, Brian confided in me that he was quite deaf and that for some time he had contemplated investing in hearing aids ("deaf aids", as they were known in England). However, they were expensive, the thought of parting with money deterred him, and anyway there was other more fundamental surgery he was planning. Beyond this he felt his life needed a fresh start, and he was determined to make a career change. Wistfully, and typically of his love for all things French, he described how much he admired the handsome and debonair actor Maurice Chevalier.

"If only," Brian said, "I had Chevalier's suavity and charm. I've got intelligence and drive. I would be unstoppable. Regardless, my plan is to get a new job and offer my experience here plus my languages to the international advertising agencies in London. They're wanting to expand in Europe when the Common Market gets going. I could be a terrific asset."

Sure enough, in a matter of weeks Brian handed in his resignation and took off for London and a promising new career. He followed through on his other fundamental intentions, too. He spent part of his increased salary on purchasing hearing aids to improve his job performance. Brian had another physical problem that led him to consult a proctologist, leading to a hemorrhoidectomy to enhance his personal comfort. He had previously kept that part of the plan to himself.

Did Brian's plans succeed? Did he enjoy a richer and more successful life? I never learned the long-term result, but before we lost touch he telephoned me soon after settling in London. He said the job was living up to expectations so far. He also let me know that his operation had an unexpected and positive result. I asked him exactly what he meant.

"Well," he said sounding none too pleased. "It cured my deafness."

"You must be overjoyed," I said.

"Actually, I'm pretty pissed," grumbled Brian. "*Mon Dieu! Je suis en colère!* I wasted all that money on those expensive bloody deaf aids. They're no damn use to me any more!"

What wonderful colleagues, so stimulating. However, they were a bit on the strange side, weren't they? I am grateful to be normal.

Top of the World

When I took up my first job it required a long move away from my home in Cornwall, at the southwestern tip of Britain, to Newcastle upon Tyne on the border with Scotland in Northumberland, the northeastern most county in England. Despite multiple new experiences to occupy my attention, I felt disoriented. The cold and windswept North Sea was much less hospitable than were the English Channel on the south coast of Cornwall where palm trees grew, and even the Atlantic Ocean on its north.

Fortunately, a kind and remarkable couple took me in. I was introduced to them by James and June Hill. James lived on the same staircase as my brother-in-law Ian Mackenzie at Cambridge. He was an engineer and worked in Gateshead, just south of the River Tyne in County Durham. Gateshead is famous for its public houses. Tynesiders, affectionately nicknamed "Geordies", claim there are more pubs in Gateshead than in all the towns put together on the Great North Road between there and London.

James' firm designed and built huge turbines for major electrical generating projects. The founder had sketched freehand a design for the turbine blade that became the core of the firm's expertise. Decades later when aero engineers used computers to design fan blades for jet engines, they were unable to make improvements. James' job took him to America to supervise a team of Geordie workmen at the Tennessee Valley Authority. When one of the team was leaving, he invited James to his going-away party, and not surprisingly, the motel room was knee deep in empty beer cans.

Through the Hills I was fortunate to meet Fred Jackson, one of the most remarkable men I have known. He was the second husband of Joan, an equally remarkable woman. Like many houses in the suburb of Gosforth, straddling the Great North Road on the northern edge of the city, theirs was large, comfortable and semi-detached with plenty of room for them, their two small daughters, their German maids, and now me. The back garden was walled, private and spacious.

Fred read economics at Cambridge and followed his father in a career as a banker. Finding it boring, he went back to his studies and became a doctor, eventually qualifying as a cardiologist. He combined working as a consultant for the National Health Scheme at the Newcastle General Hospital with running a private practice out of an office in his home. He had earned the title of doctor and later, in the English fashion, rose to the height of being addressed as "Mister" once again.

Joan married a German when she was eighteen, three weeks before the war broke out. They were honeymooning in a canoe on the Rhine when they heard the news of Germany's invasion of Poland followed by Britain's declaration of war on September 3rd, 1939. Her husband was called up into the German army, and they parted. She had no way to get back to England, and was in Germany for the duration.

Joan was tough and adaptable. She went to Hamburg to live with his family, whom she barely knew. She studied her German and became fluent. She helped out with the family's toy manufacturing business, which marketed a Radio Flyer. Joan endured danger and privation, and one can only imagine the effect on this young woman of the constant bombing, the seesawing news from the front, and the shortages of food, clothing, and medical supplies, not to mention being a British subject living with her country's enemy.

Towards the end of the war Joan received a message from her husband saying that he had been seriously wounded and invalided out of the army. He pleaded with her to go to East Germany to bring him home. She traveled through the Russian occupied zone where conditions were dreadful and the Russians soldiers cruel. Trains and buses were disrupted. There was little food or fuel. People burned their furniture to keep warm. They suffered savagely at the hands of the occupying forces. Women especially were at great risk.

After weeks of dangerous travel, much of the time in hiding, she found her husband and brought him home. The appalling discovery was that he had been faking the seriousness of his wounds in order to get out of the army. The risks she had taken appeared unjustified, but they got back to Hamburg and tried to build a life together.

While his physical injuries were less serious than he had claimed, her husband's psychological injuries were devastating. He could not relate to her or to reality and became mentally abusive to her. He would spend hours getting out of bed and dressing. He could not make the simplest decisions. He would put his shoes on and take them off, put them on again and take them off again, and on, and off, for hours.

Joan tried everything. Nothing worked. Inevitably they divorced. She returned to England and met Fred. He was kind. They married and created a happy household that they were generous in sharing. They brought an *au pair* girl from Germany to care for their two daughters. Joan kept up her German, although she sometimes mixed her English metaphors. My favorite was, "You could have knocked me down with a barge pole!"

Fred used his time and intellect in disciplined ways, prioritizing his profession, his practice, research, his family, serious music, and mountaineering, with no time for novels or popular entertainment. Under Fred's influence my youthfully arrogant view of Mozart as "pretty" was redirected into a deeper appreciation. He annotated his patients' records on file cards, along the edges of which he punched holes or slots so that he could sort categories by aligning them and poking a knitting needle through the holes. The cards with the slots dropped out and the ones with the holes were retained in the categories he had determined. This was decades before the use of computers.

He was a physical fitness nut, and his professional knowledge convinced him of the importance of exercise for heart health. Mountaineering inspired his enthusiasm, and he was prepared to accept any invitation to climb at the drop of a Tyrolean hat. In his willingness to create exercise opportunities, he took on any challenge. One day, he decided that the water pipes running beneath the back garden might have a leak, so Fred dug by hand a trench some twenty feet long by four feet wide by eight feet deep, unearthing and fixing the problem.

Soon after that, Fred invited me to join him and our mutual friend James (also a climber) on a "walk" along Hadrian's Wall. I accepted with alacrity, foreseeing no problems. Both were years older than I. Clearly delusional, I thought that walking, playing squash and occasional rugger kept me fit. The two kept a fearsome pace up hill and down dale, and there were plenty of both. It was exhausting to try and keep up, and from time to time I panted out a plea for a breather. What remained of my heart went out to the benighted Roman soldiers who piled up the stones to keep the Picts and Scots out in the first place.

A year or two later and now married, I took my wife in our sturdy little Fiat Millicento with our baby daughter Sarah on a camping trip to Scotland and the Isle of Skye. Fred told us he would be climbing with a party of Russians in the Cullin Mountains overlooking the Kyle of Lochalsh. He invited us to join them one evening in the local pub. We walked from Portree, past stacks of cut peat, and through the strange twilight that lasts all night in those northern parts. The New Zealand beekeeper Sir Edmund Hillary of Everest fame was in their party.

Fred was too modest to share how lofty the elevation of his climbing circles was, but it became clear during that evening. Thus it was less of a surprise to learn that he had been invited by the Himalayan Committee to accompany the expedition led by Dr. Mike Ward to make the first ascent on Ama Dablam in 1961. Fred was expedition doctor and also conducted physiological research to learn why the native Sherpas enjoyed superior heart health. He evaluated the connection between the rigors of living at high altitude and a low calorie diet. Unfortunately, the climax of the expedition turned into disaster when the two-man summit party was lost during their descent.

Fred later found himself in a position to invite Mike Ward to climb some of the lower peaks in the Himalayas. Here's how that came about. Fred came to know a man, a member of Lloyds, who was wealthy, well connected, and persuasive. He distracted Fred from his practice in Newcastle by asking for special favors more than once based on Fred's growing reputation as a cardiologist. The first time he called upon Fred to check on his mother who lived in Malta. She was suffering from heart problems and not doing well. Fred rescheduled his appointments and crossed to Malta to visit her.

Fred pulled off a miracle cure, although he was modest about his accomplishment. He thoroughly examined his patient and found that the local doctors had been over dosing her with digitalis. Fred took her off the drug, her condition greatly improved, and her life was happily lengthened.

Impressed, his friend called for another long distance favor. This time the journey was to Bhutan. The king was dangerously ill, and his premature death would have led to political instability. Fred could hardly refuse, and anyway it would be an opportunity for an expense paid trip back to the Himalayas. Once again he pulled off a miracle cure. The king and his advisers were delighted.

Their reward was permission to climb previously inaccessible peaks in Bhutan. Fred invited Mike Ward to join him, and their expedition was enjoyable, successful, and without mishap. As they trekked through deep snow on their return, they were met by a contingent from the palace guard, a fearsome looking group. Fred was initially concerned and thought perhaps the leaders of the tiny country had decided to protect their habitual isolation from these British interlopers. Concern turned to delight when the officer in charge produced a case of champagne, proclaimed the king's greetings, and escorted them back to the capital.

By now Fred's friend was really impressed. He announced that Fred's medical prowess had earned such deep respect that he was prepared to entrust him with a seriously important assignment that was close to his own heart. He planned to buy some racehorses in Kentucky at the Lexington yearling sales. Now the tricky thing with evaluating young horses is that it is difficult to discover critical but not uncommon heart defects. For a third time Fred rescheduled his appointments. He traveled to Kentucky to examine the horses' hearts before entering any bids. The purchases turned out well, but I don't know what their racing record was or whether Fred, who was not a gambling man, ever had the heart to take a flutter.

By then I had been transferred on what was intended to be a temporary assignment to Cincinnati in America. The good fortune was that Fred was able to stay with us on his way back to England. To digress for a moment, shortly before my transfer I had been promoted to a level where I was provided with a company car. This meant I needed to sell the Fiat. That proved hard. She was unusual in English eyes and needed work. Fred simply came forward at Joan's suggestion and bought the Fiat for her. It was typical of their kindness and generosity.

During Fred's visit we caught up with each other's doings. He showed us his marvelous slides from the Himalayas, which we shared with a friend who had also climbed there. It was one of the few times I have enjoyed someone else's vacation pictures.

The last time I saw Fred and Joan was after they had retired and we visited their remote house with beautiful views nestled in a valley deep in the Lake District in the northwest of England. Fred was surrounded by his beloved mountains. Though they lacked the grandeur of many he had climbed, he could still trek to their peaks and survey his surroundings from the top of the world. The house was a solid stone-built structure designed to withstand the bitter winter winds and snow. It was surprisingly cheap, a bargain.

The reason for the low price became apparent with the onset of twilight. A squadron of low flying Royal Air Force fighter jets roared terrifyingly through the valley. Apparently it was an ideal location to rehearse below-the-radar contour hugging formation flying. Fred and Joan were unperturbed.

"This happens every evening," Fred said calmly, "It's peaceful the rest of the time. This means it must be time for a beer. Would you like to try a pint of my home brewed?"

Ancestry

I have often wondered where I came from. Why do we dig for our roots? What is so interesting about our ancestry? Maybe it has to do with our need to address the eternal questions about the purpose of our existence, why we were put upon this earth, what makes us tick. Perhaps it helps to reinforce our sense of self worth, even of self-importance. If our forebears were people of great birth, fame, wealth, or accomplishment we could better understand ourselves, at least those parts of our makeup that were influenced by our genetics and our talents and on which we hope our environment and acquired skills have been built. We could even indulge ourselves by basking in the reflection of their glory and encouraging others to admire us.

There is the risk that fame would turn out to be notoriety, and that our forebears were thieves, vagabonds, idlers, debtors, drunkards or worse, whose careers could best be left to ignominy. This possibility presents a conundrum: to seek out our ancestry or not? The answer lies in never delegating the task of research. Keep it in the family.

If you have a family member like my wife Penny who has a painstaking ability to dig out obscure information and utilize technical knowhow, you are fortunate indeed. When such skills are combined with a wicked sense of humor then you have to watch out. You may indeed end up with a fascinating family tree that is accessible on the web, complete with not only names and dates but also photographs, birth certificates, school reports and obituaries. But if you have an older sister who was a tease in childhood, then you may suffer affectionate but embarrassing revenge in the form of information that appears to challenge your most Waspish prejudices about the purity of your genes.

In the case of my own family, my eldest sister Pam started the research, digging among family bibles, parish records, tombstones, and registries of births, marriages and deaths at Somerset House in

London where all the secrets reside. After her death, our middle sister Pat finished the job with her characteristic conscientiousness and tact. She assembled by hand complete family trees comprising multiple branches while preserving the flattering legends.

We sprang mostly from solid yeoman and artisan stock, self-improving and respectable Non-Conformists, people with positions and continuity in the Cornish villages and small towns of their birth, who insisted on educating their children. They prospered as small businessmen. We do know that our surname, Hoskin, was derived from the Cornish language word "Os" for osier, or willow twig. So our ancestors were apparently the "kin" or people who dwelled by the reeds, and possibly were basket weavers, entrepreneurs long ago.

There were also legends of genteel blood supported by ancient photographs of great grandparents with refined features. These may have arisen from <u>visitations on the other side of the blanket</u> not recorded in official documents and buried with their bones.

I am gratified to have passed my middle names on to my grandson, the seventh generation called John Collins. Apparently the Collinses on my father's side were somehow connected to the Runnalls on my mother's side, which led to the introduction and eventual marriage of my parents, despite growing up in towns twenty-four miles apart. We are not sure of the connection, and it remains undocumented. Happily for my sisters' and my sanity, this is not a case of first cousins marrying.

One of the myths is that, like many in Cornwall, the dark-haired, brown-eyed Runnalls family was the result of interminging with survivors of the Spanish Armada. Lo and behold, my sister discovered an early parish record showing Runnalls spelled with the Spanish tilde over a single "n" as in "ñ". Furthermore, I recently had my DNA analyzed, and while most of my ancestry was from southwest Britain, 19% of my genes are traced to the Iberian peninsula. Now all that may not be proof to a genealogist but it's certainly enough to perpetuate romance.

Things turned out less romantically with my great uncle, Harry Oke Hoskin. His silver pocket watch was passed down to my father. It has a handsome engraved face and a little key that winds it up and adjusts its hands. Harry was a missionary, and we grew up believing that he had been boiled and eaten by cannibals in Africa while steadfastly proclaiming his faith.

My brother-in-law, a professional historian, researched the records of the Methodist Missionary Society and discovered that Great Uncle Harry had in fact served in the Caribbean. His death was on the order of chivalry. When a lady missionary in his party fell overboard, he dived in to rescue her with more gallantry than discretion, since he could not swim. Panicked, she resisted his efforts, and he drowned. She survived, borne up by the pocket of air trapped in her voluminous crinoline skirts. It was a romantic end in its own way, although not quite as compelling as stoic endurance in the devoted service of his Lord.

Great Uncle Harry typified the enthusiasm of many of our family, and indeed many Cornish people, to seek excitement around the world. I have distant cousins everywhere, from New Zealand to Canada, from Africa to America, and even some who emigrated to Australia under their own steam and not as criminals sent off by the crown.

One of the traits I also inherited from my ancestors was entrepreneurialism. The first manifestation I remember, albeit in microeconomic form, was at the age of seven. The circus came to our small town offering the allure of wild beasts and wilder performers, from lion tamers to bareback riders, from sword swallowers to knife throwers, from tight rope walkers to acrobats, and of course the clowns.

They arrived as I was at the bottom of the garden, performing my customary summer service of checking the ripeness of my father's raspberries. With a mouthful of deep red sweetness, I watched the colorful wagons snake into the field behind our house. Soon a gaggle of children collected and stood fascinated as the performers set out their caravans and arranged the traveling cages of the lions and tigers into a colorful menagerie. The climax came when the roustabouts put up the big top with the help of their intelligent and beautifully trained elephants.

"Sir Robert Fossett's Famous International Circus" entertained the townsfolk and enthralled their children for three days. Then it was time to pack up and move on to the next town. We kids were allowed to help, as long as we didn't get in the way. Too soon it was all over, and a sense of letdown followed, but not for long. In the corner of the field where the elephants had been lay an awe-inspiring and steaming pile of manure, decorated with partially digested bamboo leaves. I spotted a *business opportunity.*

Borrowing my father's garden fork, I pulled my barrow towards the mound and filled it with this golden bonanza. I was used to being up close and personal with cows, so it was not a particularly unpleasant task. I tugged my barrow along to our neighbor Mr. Oliver's house. He was a keen vegetable gardener, and it took mere moments of visualizing unprecedented fecundity to persuade him to invest a penny a forkful in this exotic manure. Encouraged, I repeated this success with several neighbors until my supply ran out.

All went well until a few days later. Mr. Oliver's entire patch of new cabbage plants turned yellow. They were on their way to the great compost heap in the sky. He was kind enough not to ask, but I felt I had to give him his money back. I avoided the other gardens. My dream of a national chain of elephant manure suppliers rotted away.

All was not lost however; there were lessons to be learned. Regarding your family tree: it is important to keep in mind the purpose of the enterprise, which is self-glorification and the preservation of selected myths. Do not sacrifice familial flattery on the altar of accuracy. *Never* entrust research to an expert; and keep the creation and publishing of the tree and any flattering pruning firmly within the family.

Regarding entrepreneurial ventures: it is vital to research your product before going to market. Be wary of the temptations of choosing large units of production to expand your manufacturing. You may end up magnifying your mistakes. Guard against unbridled enthusiasm. Finally, never offer a money back guarantee, even when your asking price is low.

Gustatory Defeat

Some years ago I traveled from my new home in Cincinnati back to England on a business trip, choosing late November when airfares were at bargain levels. It was a nostalgic visit, bringing back earlier memories of a projected journey from Lands End to John o' Groats, the extreme tips of Britain. I didn't actually make that trip, but the idea felt like an appropriate symbol for the transition from my birthplace in Cornwall to my new home after graduating and starting work in Northumberland.

I had forgotten how bleak the extreme north of England could be in November. The climate explained why the beautiful countryside supported more sheep than people. The sheep came with woolly coats. I had been invited to stay at the home of a business colleague. I had looked forward to once again gazing at the dry-stone walls and the magnificent rolling fells as he drove us west along the Roman road.

My host drove me to his home. However, I could not enjoy the views; it was three in the afternoon and already dark. The ice covering the windshield was impenetrable to the defroster. My field of vision was further limited by the heavy snow and wisps of fog. The wind howling from the North Sea had blanketed the walls with deep drifts. Ah yes, I remember it well.

It was a wonderful house, just off the Military Road and south of Hadrian's Wall. It was Georgian, of the solid, rustic variety, built of local stone. Like many farm houses in those parts, it was sited suspiciously close to a partly ruined ancient Roman mile castle, whose components had been put to more recent use than that of the legions. We parked the car in a former cow byre under a roof of three-inch thick stone slabs hooked to the rafters with the rib bones of sheep. We ploughed across feet of crisp snow to the back door, the cold penetrating the heavy Crombie greatcoat that I had inherited from my father.

I staggered into the kitchen and gratefully thawed my backside against the Aga stove, enough to risk taking off my overcoat. Some deep set dog lover's instinct led me to befriend the two Jack Russell terriers, not my favorite breed, that yapped a hysterical welcome. I was reluctant to leave the kitchen, which was the warmest room in the house. When I was shown to my unheated bedroom I was tempted to leave immediately and accompany Shackleton to the Antarctic in order to warm up. Instead I would stay up as late as possible, add my overcoat to the blankets, and smuggle table scraps from dinner to bribe the Jack Russells to sleep in the bed with me.

Our hostess announced that she was celebrating my arrival with a dinner party, and promised interesting guests. My host prepared us for being charming by dispensing generous doses of a rare single malt Scotch whisky in their drawing room. It took me only a moment to forego my acquired American habit of asking for ice. The whisky was already chilled in the bottle on the sideboard, and if it warmed up in one's fingers it would be a simple matter to wave it in the air just inside the window to bring its temperature close to freezing.

I thought at first glance that it was a bay window. Closer inspection revealed that the window frame was actually set in the outer part of a three-foot thick stone wall. The depth of the wall effectively reduced the coating of ice on its inside to a mere sprinkling of frost. There had been no effete concession to the thinned blood of the transatlantic visitor such as double-glazing. The ancient hand-blown glass panes rattled in their frames and the wind from the moors beyond Hadrian's Wall whistled through the leaks between the glass and the aged cracked and shriveled putty.

On the temperate side of the room was a blazing coal fire. My hostess hospitably insisted that I take the armchair set inches from the hearth. As the evening wore on, the arteries in my left thigh bubbled as the blood approached boiling point. My right leg, however, froze so deeply that my knee joint operated only with great effort. Even my host's promise of the lubricating powers of his Scotch failed to do the trick, although on reflection he may have been referring to the effect on my tongue rather than my knee.

The guests arrived, removed protective clothing, thawed, and joined us. The most interesting were a middle-aged gentleman and woman and a much younger lady, who was strikingly attractive. They were introduced as an Englishman and his wife who had just returned from an assignment in the States, bringing his American secretary with them. He explained that he was an academic who had spent a couple of years at an American university teaching and doing research in his specialty, which was the treatment of sewage. He also explained that actually the young woman was not really his secretary. There were plenty of highly qualified secretaries in England. She was in fact his mistress, Barbara.

Barbara was delightful, intelligent and vivacious. Since our hostess deemed us both not to be hardy, she and I ended up sitting together by the fire on opposite sides of the fireplace. We chatted and sparred and jousted, with me clearly getting the best of it, serving one ace after another. She tried, but simply could not match my urbane British wit, at least in my critical opinion, now inspired by further infusions of the single malt. Eventually I felt sorry for her as she seemed to surrender and lapse into virtual silence. She was rescued by our hostess announcing dinner, but as fate would have it we were seated next to each other.

The polished antique dining table glowed in the light of candles. The food and wine were resplendent. The cockaleekie soup, a regional treat, was warming and tasty. The main course comprised huge slices of a traditional English steak and kidney pie, crowned by perfectly browned pastry, served with generous helpings of home grown vegetables, all my favorites, roast potatoes, peas, carrots, parsnips and Brussels sprouts, complete with horseradish sauce. It was a feast worth making a transatlantic pilgrimage for. It was accompanied by an ancient claret, poured unstintingly by our host.

The conversation sparkled around the table. Despite my earlier intentions of gallantry I could not dampen my enjoyment; I resumed my one sided contest with Barbara. Serve, volley, backhand, advantage me. The plates were emptied. The guests were replete. The wine glasses were refilled. Our hostess promised to follow the repast with a premature Christmas pudding enriched with brandy butter. But before clearing the table she offered seconds of the magnificent entrée. Each diner in turn graciously refused.

Now it is not that I obviously needed feeding up, but when it came to my turn, I appreciatively said, "I would love some more, it's delicious, so savory, thank you." I alone of the company passed my scoured plate.

Glances came my way, chatter dried up, followed by one of those unending silences that falls upon a group when something is about to happen that one would prefer to pass unnoticed. My dinner companion said, in a distinctly enunciated whisper to our hostess that reverberated across the mahogany table surface, "It's like feeding buns to an elephant!"

Game, set, match. Barbara, I salute you.

Special Relationship

As a Briton living in America, I have from time to time found myself in the role of unofficial volunteer ambassador to both countries, recounting or explaining the customs, culture, history and often language of each to the other. I usually manage to perform my self-appointed duties in a state of suitably diplomatic sangfroid, although occasionally I have found it difficult, as one might express it in more contemporary terms, to keep my cool.

I remember a time during a visit to my native land being introduced at a party to a formidable dowager who languidly greeted me with, "Oh, so you live in the colonies now," in the tone of voice that expected a polite titter or at least a jolly agreement. I was not amused. In fact I was really irritated. I had become sick and tired of the condescending and frankly snobbish attitudes of a certain type of English person towards my adopted home.

I coolly asked, "Exactly what do you mean by that?"

She blundered along with, "Well, you know, red Indians, cowboys, loud ties, bright lights and noisy television on all day long and no culture and all that jolly sort of rot, don't you know!"

Usually I barely manage a stumbling inanity in responding to this kind of outrageous remark and then wish I could rerun the conversation later after ruminating for a while to compose a devastating answer. For once quickness of passion compensated for slowness of thought.

I riposted with, "Actually, what I know and have learned to deeply respect is that Americans are full of kindness and hospitality, energy and inventiveness, enterprise and adventure, ambition and zest, generosity and good humor, willingness to learn and to change for the better. They have learned to treat their native people, as well as new Americans from all over the world, with more respect and with consideration. Cowboys are about as common as gamekeepers or thatchers. Loud ties went out long ago, and the people I know enjoy good music and watch the BBC, a little.

"The American *people*, not just their government, support symphony orchestras, museums, art galleries, ballet companies and theaters. They do it personally with their own money and most of all with their volunteer energy, not just in their major cities but in smaller cities and towns all over their country. They are proud of their varied landscape, and they are proud of their short history, and they support their preservation. Americans of all stripes visit their landmarks in enthusiastic droves."

"But . . ." she interrupted.

I pressed on. "Furthermore, and fortunately for you and me, Americans have taken over the role of world leadership that Britain is too worn out and too impoverished to sustain. They have certainly pursued national interests, but they have also given with unceasing generosity to those in need all over the globe as a matter of moral duty as well as in times of crisis."

I drew breath and asked her, "May I get you a cucumber sandwich?"

"Well, thank you, but I don't think so," she gasped. And fled.

Some time later back home in Cincinnati one of those occasions came about that led to unexpected efforts and pleasures. My wife and I had introduced to our social circle Scottish dancing (the Eightsome Reel, the Strathspey, the Dashing White Sergeant, the Sir Roger de Coverly) as well as English Edwardian dancing (the Lancers, the Quadrilles, the Gavotte), and we met regularly in each others homes to learn, practice and simply enjoy ourselves. One of our hosts had a Scots houseguest who was visiting to promote a tour of a British Military Tattoo throughout North America.

Brigadier Alistair Maclean, Queen's Own Sutherland Highlanders, had produced the Tattoo at the Edinburgh Festival. A "tattoo" in this context is a very special traditional form of military entertainment. He was bringing a magnificent show with the Royal Marines band, bands of the Scots Guards and the Scots Greys regiments, Scottish dancers, a motorcycle display team, *and* the James

Bond Aston Martin. It was booked to tour forty-three cities in the U.S. and Canada; but not Cincinnati.

I unwisely commented, "That's unfortunate."

He said, "That's easily overcome. All we need is someone here to promote it. *You* are volunteered." The habit of command fell easily to Brigadier Maclean, and my objections were firmly, if courteously, swept away.

A few days later I arranged for him to meet the president of the local chapter of the anglophile English-Speaking Union. After an amiable lunch at the Queen City Club, Maclean's combination of firmness and charm led to an agreement that the chapter would sponsor the event. I unwittingly paid the price of being elected *in absentia* as the new president of the chapter with the major responsibility of organizing and promoting the event. But that is another story, as is the story of the coincidence of the Tattoo's Pipe Major turning out to be Kilgour, who had been my brother-in-law's batman in the Scots Guards and whom I had met when he piped at my sister's wedding.

As we were chatting in the lobby after lunch, I saw John Dalzell. He had recently been appointed editor of the new *Cincinnati Magazine*. Recognizing that friendly media coverage was going to be critical to success, I seized the opportunity to build a warm relationship between the two of them.

"John, this is Brigadier Maclean of the Queen's Own Sutherland Highlanders. He is bringing the Military Tattoo from the Edinburgh Festival to Cincinnati. Brigadier Maclean, this is John Dalzell. He is proud of his Scottish ancestry, and he plays the bagpipes."

"Harrumph," said Maclean. He was not being charming. The conversation aborted at launch, and John said his goodbyes. Once out of earshot, Maclean said to me, "What did you say that chap's name is?"

"Dalzell," I replied.

"And he's proud of his Scottish ancestry?" queried Maclean.

"Yes," I replied.

"And he lets them call him Dal-Zell?" he demanded.

"Yes," I replied. "Americans aren't really up on things like pronouncing it 'Dee-yell', and it's hard to keep on explaining it."

"And he plays the pipes, and he's proud of his Scottish ancestry and he let's them call him DAL-ZELL," said a now apoplectic Maclean.

"Yes," I said apologetically. Maclean's response was emphatic.

"Bastard!"

I enjoy that story and must confess I have told it more than once. Oscar Wilde once said, "We really have everything in common with America nowadays except, of course, language."

I've often thought that the English joy in pronouncing names other than the way they are written makes a characteristic contribution to the confusion: Marjoribanks *Marchbanks;* Featherstonehaugh *Fanshaw;* Urquhart *Erkhart;* Menzies *Mingys;* Smythe *Smith;* Montefiore *Montyfury*); and indeed Maclean *Maclane.* American amazement at the quaint customs of the Brits is part of what keeps the special relationship going.

Years later my wife Penny and I were in Vermont having dinner with friends, including Mrs. Mackenzie, the elderly mother of our hostess. She too was proud of her Scottish ancestry. While I am always willing to work the conversation around to fit what I want to say, on this occasion there was a natural segue. Mrs. Mackenzie was a rewarding audience. She listened to my story with rapt attention.

After I delivered the punch line she asked coyly, "Did you say Alistair Maclean? Did you say he was in the Queen's Own Sutherland Highlanders? Are you sure?"

"Yes," I said.

"I remember Alistair Maclean very well," she said. "I spent a wonderful summer with Alistair in Scotland when I was a girl of eighteen." Her eyes were sparkling, with youthful enthusiasm, and very slightly, she blushed.

And that, I would venture to suggest, was a very special relationship.

Memories While Memory Lasts ☙ ☙ page 93

Gentlemen's Game

Puberty's onset in my son some decades ago challenged my skills and indeed patience as a father. Flooding new hormones transformed a mostly well-behaved boy into a brat who amused himself by teasing and beating up on his sisters and sometimes resisting parental instructions. Our children were very different.

One evening after dinner provided the perfect illustration. We were all sitting on the sofa watching television. As the program ended our eldest Sarah said, "It's time for me to go up to my room and do my homework."

Their mother said, "Yes, up you all go, bedtime, come on Nick."

Our middle child said angrily, "I don't want to. You're always picking on me, just because I'm the only boy," and stormed off. Our youngest Tori said nothing and imperceptibly scrunched deeper into her corner of the sofa.

As the next program ended my wife said, "Tori, what are you still doing up? You should have been in bed long ago."

They have not changed all that much over the years, although I am glad to report that Nick's behavior proved to be a passing phase. At the time, however, something urgently had to be done.

My work as a management consultant introduced me to Systems Thinking, based on the concept that the component parts of a system can be best understood through their relationships with each other and other systems, rather than in isolation. To fully understand why a problem or element occurs and persists, one must understand the part in relation to the whole, and identify the inputs that are transformed into outputs.

Aha! Herein lay the solution to my parenting problem. I had tried reasoning and even discipline with my son, but the output was merely hardening of his resistance, doubtless stemming from stubbornness inherited from his mother's side.

Gentlemen's Game 🙢 🙢 page 94

The answer was clear. I had to construct a new system. If I wanted different outputs, I simply had to create different inputs. If I could provide excessive amounts of physical exercise for him, then the resultant exhaustion would leave him with insufficient energy to bother his sisters. And ideally he would learn lifelong lessons, too.

So I drew on my experience of growing up in England and created a system for American boys around my new home in Ohio to play Rugby football.

Now, Rugby is a fine game, invented to prepare young gentlemen for the rough and tumble of life, instilling in them values such as teamwork, sportsmanship, friendship and the amateur ideal. Its invention occurred at a fashionable boys' boarding school and was not exactly systematic. It just happened on a never-to-be-forgotten day in 1823 at Rugby School in England when William Webb Ellis "with a fine disregard of the laws of football as played in his day picked up the ball and ran with it".

Rugby football is an international game; my young players could gain a worldview beyond the parochial bounds of games played only in America. For the Rugby World Cup the number of countries admitted to the preliminary tournament is whittled down to 96, organized in four regions to qualify for 20 places in the final stage. In the recent cup competition, the U.S.A. was beaten early by Samoa (population 193,000). In the final, nearly 90,000 spectators (one third more than attended the Super Bowl) watched New Zealand beat Argentina to become world champions.

For my purposes, football played according to the Rugby code had many advantages over its sports cousins. Compared with Association Football, or "Soccer" as it has been abbreviated, Rugby has teams of 15 players rather than 11, so you can exercise almost 40% more hormonal young bodies. It also better simulates combat. Compared with its derivative American Football, it requires fewer resources: no expensive gladiator clothes, only one referee and two "touch judges" rather than a committee of officials elaborately dressed like zebras, one whistle rather than a bunch of yellow dusters that get lost and have to be replaced, and no time-outs, so the players get tired more quickly. The overwhelming advantage is that parents have no idea what the rules are or what is going on, so they are too confused to criticize the coach.

What did it take to get started? A ball, a whistle, a field, a referee, some coaches and, for those in the habit if dressing up in specialist costumes in order to exercise, some Rugby shirts. Oh, we also needed players and, not incidentally, other teams to play against.

The proper oval ball was provided by a visitor from England. I already had a whistle for training bird dogs. One just had to blow it differently to avoid the players going on point at the sound. I persuaded the village Recreation Commission to provide fields with goal posts. I could get started by refereeing myself, although I quickly realized I was out of date on the laws. We could add more referees when needed.

The local Rugby clubs were more than willing to help coach, seeing not only an opportunity to proselytize the Rugby culture but also to recruit future club members. Many members were British ex-pats with a deeply ingrained love for the game. Fortuitously, Rugby shirts had just become a fashion, so authentic supplies of tough striped cotton shirts with rubber buttons at the neck were readily available.

That was everything we needed to get started. Except for the players. I already knew where one could be persuaded to shirt up. We just needed fourteen more for my team and then fifteen others to play against.

Fortunately, a system was emerging in which I could participate as an influencer: kids' soccer, then in its infancy. Soccer was promoted by parents at the community level through local recreation commissions and then introduced to schools. I could join in spreading a brand of football not yet popular in America and later make the leap to promoting my true love, the gentlemanly Rugby code. This became the path I pursued.

It was amazing how suburban kids and more importantly their parents, embraced the working-class game of soccer. All soccer involved was chasing a round ball around a field. But at least it offered exercise, even to less athletic kids who were neither gargantuan nor masochistic enough to qualify for American football.

Though lacking profound appreciation of the finer points of the game, parents could grasp the basic principles easily enough to scream conflicting instructions from the sidelines. Furthermore, girls could play which, while heretical to the rest of the world, appealed to the American egalitarian tradition and also got the girls out of the house on Saturday mornings with their brothers.

There was a shortage of coaches, so when I volunteered I was welcomed. My experience of playing soccer was limited to ages nine to thirteen, but that made me a comparative expert. So it made sense for now to sign up my son for a soccer team and burn off some of his energy for the time being that way. Coaching kids appealed to me. We all like to feel that we will leave something behind when we move on to our next existence. Perhaps my immortality could lie in my positive influence on the values and fitness of future citizens; something to be remembered by.

I paired up with a dedicated father who knew nothing of the game, so we agreed to divide up our duties. We put him in charge of moral rectitude while I focused on imparting soccer skills and tactics. There were some aspects that I felt he overdid, but he embraced my British ideas of sportsmanship and fair play. It was important to set the bloody little ball hogs a good example so that we could impress their parents with our positive influence on their pampered offspring.

We taught them to offer their opponents a helping hand if they knocked them over. We discouraged tripping when the referee wasn't looking. We imbued them with an attitude that healthy enjoyment in the open air was fundamentally more important than competitiveness and winning. From a practical standpoint, that mitigated a lot of disappointment, since our team's lack of athletic prowess meant they usually lost.

We were blessed with one or two boys with a modicum of fitness and coordination who at least grasped the fundamental principle that they were supposed to kick the ball towards their opponents' goal. One blue-eyed, fair-haired lad was really talented, good enough to play at the key position of striker in the middle of our offense. But despite his angelic appearance he was conceited and selfish, the ultimate ball hog. He needed to be taught a lesson in team spirit.

Halfway through our perfect season without a win to our name, I decided to bench him at the beginning of the game. He pestered me from the sidelines throughout the first quarter. I relentlessly stuck to my principles. However, when we were down seven to nil, my fellow coach prevailed, and I sent him on the field but demoted him to the outside right position, away from the action.

Our supporters were heartened, and their shouts of encouragement grew louder even though it was still too early in their acquisition of expertise to be more constructive than cries of "Kick it!"; "Foul!"; "Don't bunch up!"; "Kill him!" They had not yet achieved the level of moral rectitude being drilled into their sons.

Excitingly, the ball went up as well as down the field. But our angelic star was too far from the action to convert good intentions into goals. I could see his impatience growing. Then his moment arrived.

At one of those intervals of stillness when the most raucous of crowds falls silent, he yelled from across the field in a perfect English accent, "Why don't you bastards pass *me* the bloody ball, goddammit!" Where could *that* vocabulary have come from?

The silence continued. My fellow coach was nowhere to be seen. He must have sensed that his battle for moral rectitude was irretrievably lost. Everyone looked at me. I don't remember how the game ended, but I did sense a turning point.

Somehow several of the players got the point. Soccer is a team game. Individual players succeed to the extent they contribute to the team's success. Despite the embarrassing moment, I decided not to turn over my coaching duties to someone more suitable but to push for better soccer than ever. During our next game the players gelled into something resembling a team. They passed the ball to each other. They supported each other in defense. They ran into open spaces in attack. They brought the ball under control and kicked it with accuracy and finesse, and they didn't bunch up. And they won!

At last we had the opportunity for a victory celebration over hamburgers and Cokes at MacDonald's. I rode the euphoria by telling them about the joys of Rugby, moving my hidden agenda along. In my car on the way home their questions were flowing and their interest growing.

Apparently one of them told the story to his mother. Some years later she spoke to me at a church gathering, and I asked after her son who had joined the ranks of the fine young men I had influenced and who had gone on to play Rugby at college.

She recalled her son's account of that car ride when he asked me the difference between soccer players and "rugger" players. At just that moment, the digestive system of one of his teammates had been overcome by a surfeit of onion rings and the car was filled with an unmistakable aroma. I had replied: "Rugby players don't fart". So much for immortality.

It was time to move the Rugby ball down the field; time to get teams together. With the soccer players as nucleus, I set up meetings to show potential recruits a classic film of "The Great Match" about the historic contest between the Barbarians and All Blacks.

The Barbarians were a select side made up of international players from Britain's four home countries who were invited to play against visiting touring sides from other countries at Twickenham, the home of English international Rugby. The All Blacks, or Kiwis, were the international side from New Zealand. It was said in respectful tones in pubs around the land that whereas the British played rugger to keep fit, the Kiwis kept fit to play rugger.

The Kiwis' reputation for power and speed preceded them: a huge pack, skillful half backs, fast three-quarter backs, and a full back who never missed a tackle and kicked with length and accuracy. A daunting adversary faced the "Barbars", whose mission was to demonstrate open Rugby.

I started the film with pride, only to be greeted with hoots of derision. It was in black and white, and my sophisticated audience was scornful. What kind of old fashioned game were they being shown? But their jeers turned to cheers as the closely fought contest ranged continuously from one end of the field to the other.

Then came the climax. The Kiwis kicked the ball ahead to the Barbar full back, right on his goal line. Conventional tactics called for a defensive kick for touch to recapture some ground to create a "line-out" set piece and give the beleaguered Barbars breathing room to regroup.

Instead, like his predecessor William Webb Ellis, the Barbar fullback picked up the ball and ran with it.

In Rugby the forward pass is illegal. The ball can only be passed backwards, and only the man with the ball can be tackled; there is no blocking. Seeing the situation, the Barbars ran behind the full back so he could pass to them. The pack formed a phalanx and ran down the field, closely passing to each other before they could be tackled. The speedier backs ran back in support, before the Kiwis could counter the attack, and carried the ball almost the entire length of the field.

As the last defender ran to tackle his man, the Barbar lofted it over his head to his wing three-quarter who ran around the wrong-footed Kiwi and scored the winning try. All fifteen Barbars had handled the ball in a magnificent display of open Rugby. It was indeed a great match.

Questions followed cheers. How can we get to play? How can we learn the rules? Can we have our own Rugby shirts? Wouldn't we get injured without helmets and padding? It was hard for them to grasp that football helmets cause injuries and that Rugby players avoid hurting their heads by not spear tackling. The boys' commitment showed when they asked what to call their team? Since they had to travel to various fields, they settled on the "Nomads". I had some concerns that the cheer "Go Nomads" might lead to an unfortunate spoonerism, but let it pass.

Then these avid pursuers of materialism wondered how much professionals got paid and whether there were college scholarships. The local universities had Rugby clubs with fixtures throughout the region, as did a growing number of community clubs, so I assured them they could play after high school.

I had to explain that at that time the gentlemen's version of the game was amateur. I pointed out that people played for the love of the game with two objectives: to make lifelong friendships and to work up a thirst. The social life of the adult players after the game centered on the clubhouse bar, singing the traditional Rugby songs and quenching a well-earned thirst.

The old established English club to which I used to belong had playing fields for four teams, including the "Wanderers" who were too old to play for a representative side but enjoyed the game too much to hang up their boots. There was a well-equipped clubhouse with all of the essentials including a changing room with two huge tiled square bath tubs, one for each team to clean up after the game. The water turned an unhygienic shade of dull purple from the addition of sweat, blood and mud from fifteen happily exhausted bodies.

There was a comfortable and tastefully decorated ladies lounge as well as a steel and concrete reinforced bar with soundproofing where the men welcomed their visitors and celebrated after the game. Their celebration was not about winning (although one side usually did) but rather about camaraderie. There was conversation and a great deal of hearty choral singing of a kind in which the ladies were not invited to join.

Fast forward in time and space and back to the Nomads. We were at last ready to start practicing Rugby. The local club players were eager to coach and participate in scrimmages. They proved to be excellent role models. They joined our boys and networked among their friends to spread the word. We staged an exhibition game, and bumper stickers helped spread the word: "Support your local hooker"; "Give blood, play Rugby"; and "It takes leather balls to play Rugby".

Soon other boys' teams were formed and by the end of the season there were twelve school clubs playing against each other. Our boys recruited the football stars from their schools, but that rarely worked out because they lacked the stamina to keep up in a game played continuously for two forty-minute halves with one five minute break at half-time. And they rarely adapted to the tactical improvisation of the Rugby code.

After a couple of seasons the team matured with enough skill to participate in the Mid-West Colts Tournament for sixteen teams of boys under eighteen. The Nomads traveled from their wealthy Cincinnati suburb to Chicago, supported by several parents. They played their hearts out on the pristine fescue of the New Trier School sports fields. The party afterwards in a Lakeshore mansion was an eye opener to a level of wealth they had not seen, capped by several of our players riding in the brand new Cadillac given to their host's captain by his father so he could attract girls. It was not an opportunity to revisit moral rectitude and the amateur ideal, but a cracking good time was had by all.

Many of them kept up their Rugby when they went on to college, where they were welcomed for their playing experience. I was thrilled to be greeted by several of them home for vacations. They shared their joy about playing and partying with friends made in high school and now scattered among various colleges. Many of them went on to play on club teams, and some went on to be selected for representative regional teams. One or two had international trials with the American Eagles.

Nowadays, my kids' connection with their high school days is through twenty-fifth reunions, or later. But they bring back from their old friends stories of the days when the boys learned to play Rugby football and of the friendships they have maintained over the years. It may be stretching it a bit to think of that as immortality. However that may be, it is gratifying to be stopped on the street, at a bar or elsewhere by a now grown man who remembers when he was a boy, and I was his coach.

And maybe getting boys at twelve schools playing a game with strange traditions was creating an over-elaborate system in order to exhaust a twelve year-old boy who was bothering his sisters. However, it helped that boy and his sisters be the great friends that they have become as they have created their own families.

But for me it continues to give deep satisfaction in having had positive input into the lives of boys who have grown into manhood, where the output incorporates their cherishing friendship, camaraderie, sportsmanship, teamwork, fair play, a view of the world at large, and appreciating the amateur tradition that values doing well things that have nothing to do with money.

LUGOT

Divorce is not nice. It hurts. There is never a good time for it. As even the unhappy couple in their nineties learned when they went to their priest for counseling. "Why now?" he asked. Their answer: "We wanted to wait until the children were dead."

My entirely sensible advice is to take your time, do not make any precipitate or irreversible moves; avoid commitments; try not to hurt others more than you can help; don't involve, recruit or bore other people; and trust that eventually things may get better. Though a monastery may seem like a good idea, consider the possibility that you may not be regarded as a suitable candidate and probably won't be accepted. Anyway, it's a bit late in life to start being a novice, even though that may be uncomfortably close to the truth. So maintain your friendships and don't turn down invitations to parties. Oh, and keep your poetry to yourself.

I leased a bachelor apartment for one year. I toyed with the possibility of five or ten years, but maybe some day I would want to live somewhere less punitive. I accepted invitations from the kind and the curious. I kept in touch with old friends, including one whose birthday was the same as my mother's. Being the sentimental type, I had called Penny annually for many years, just to wish her well and exchange news of our families.

This year there was a lot of news. I told Penny about my impending divorce. She kindly offered to give me advice since she had recently gained a lot of experience of the state herself. I thanked her but said I was getting advice from experts. She said that anyway I could call if I needed to talk, and if I was lonely I could come and visit for the weekend and meet her beau. I promised I would call next year.

It was at least a couple of weeks before I called Penny again. I didn't want to appear eager. She was glad to talk but was in a bit of a hurry because she was getting ready for a trip to England with her father. I wondered why, and she explained that she was considering moving to England to live. That seemed a bit radical to me, but she had got tired of the grey winters of northern New York and felt it was time for a change. Actually, Penny was considering several options including New York City, Boston and Washington. I thought they sounded pretty wintry grey too, but she was also considering Florida, all places she had lived before and where she had kept up with friends.

I asked her whether she had considered coming back to Cincinnati where she had lived for several years with her ex-husband and, indeed, where we had become friends as couples.

I first saw Penny across a crowded room at a party after the symphony. I had a strange feeling that I had known her before, perhaps in a former life. It was a memorable moment, a profoundly significant experience for me. She has no recollection of it whatsoever.

Penny wondered why on earth she would come back here to the Midwest. After all, she had lost touch with all but a few of her old friends in the thirteen years since she had moved, so whom would she spend time with and find interesting? Drawing upon depths of rarely employed self-control, I waited for her to answer her own question. After the silence became unbearable I took a sip of G&T to wet my dried up vocal cords and raise my risk tolerance level. Well, there is always me, I suggested. Huh, she said with less than her usual eloquence.

Emboldened, I suggested that I could invite a few old friends to my, by now semi-permanent, bachelor pad. They would be delighted to catch up with her and surely one would put her up. I could even arrange a couple of job interviews and help her network. So we scheduled a weekend after she got back from her trip to England, and I went ahead and sent out invitations.

Her arrival date approached, but I had heard nothing confirming arrangements. Perhaps she had forgotten. Perhaps she had decided to stay in England. I called. Well, Penny said, she had changed her mind and anyway she wasn't sure I was serious about the invitation, and was I fully divorced yet? I wondered what my divorce status had to do with the price of beans. After all, we were just old friends, and she certainly wasn't coming just to see me. But she wanted to give nobody any possible reasons for jumping to conclusions, not that anyone around here would ever gossip. But I had to admit that the divorce had a short while to be finalized. Party already arranged, we nevertheless reinstituted the visit to coincide with the May Festival and she arranged to stay with a mutual woman friend.

She did arrive and entertained a group of us at a familiar Ohio riverboat restaurant. She amusingly reminisced about old times and charmingly conversed about her disillusionment with men and her determination to remain unmarried for the rest of her life. Apparently her recent relationship was disintegrating. I allowed as how that seemed a bit drastic but, speaking for myself, I was certainly up for at least five years of monasticism. She and I later also talked about how we shared a limited tolerance for small talk at cocktail parties, the times we ended up sitting in a corner in an island of serious conversation, and the time we purloined a bottle of Scotch from our host's bar and carried it off to the tree house in the garden.

This conversation reminded me of another past dinner party when Penny provided the entertainment. We were sitting at the table during the finale of a feast, drinking coffee and sipping after-dinner liqueurs, allowing the pleasures of the evening to sink in. Penny noticed that one man had nodded off over his Benedictine. Having previously seen our host's children's pony through the French windows, she slipped out with another guest, an old friend from her Baltimore days, rode the pony wearing only its halter into the room, and positioned its muzzle next to the guest's face. The pony snorted, the guest started, the Benedictine spilled, and the party broke up in giggles.

It had rained and she and her friend had muddied their bare feet so repaired to our hostess's pride, her new bidet, to rinse off. The horrified hostess went to use her bathroom and finding a man and a woman with their feet in her bidet required some minutes of recovery before she rejoined her guests.

Meanwhile, back with Penny during her visit to Cincinnati. On Friday evening I took her to the May Festival, and the intermission was replete with incident. She crept up stealthily behind a rather proper old friend and goosed him, as she had done many times before she left Cincinnati. To her delight, the familiar blush ran up the back of his neck and without turning his head, he spoke her name with warm recognition. Hugs and a warm conversation followed. Then we ran into a couple coming down the broad staircase from the circle into the foyer who were equally delighted to see Penny. They invited her to their big anniversary party in a few weeks and said I should bring her. I had actually been thinking of taking someone else but it did not seem the time or place to go into that.

On Saturday we had a cheerful reunion lunch with my daughter Sarah who had gone to college in Vermont. My family and I had often visited Penny and her family in upper New York on our way driving up north or back. Just as I picked up the check and was about to suggest a tour of old haunts, she looked at her watch and announced that she would miss her plane if we didn't hurry. I said I had assumed she was staying for the weekend. But she had places to go, people to see, things to do.

I didn't let my Saturday May Festival tickets go unused. However, I did call Penny on Monday and inquired whether she had arrived safely. She seemed to think (actually she made it perfectly clear) that if I had cared in the least I would have called before then. It became apparent that it would be wise for me to continue to maintain my local friendships in the broadest possible way.

So the following weekend I went to a wedding. Big tent, big crowd, big band, big supply of champagne, fun dancing partners. I partook to the full of everything that was offered. After some trial and error I arrived back at my bachelor apartment in the wee small hours. But the night seemed too young to end just yet. So I called Penny. She sleepily wondered what the hell I wanted at that hour. I told her I wanted to marry her, which seemed like a pretty good idea at the time. She said yes, provided I cut the conversation short and let her go back to sleep.

At an ungodly hour close to noon the following day Penny took her turn to wake me. Her son sleeping in the room next to hers had asked at breakfast who had called in the middle of the night and what they wanted. Ever practical, he urged clarification. So she demanded whether I was serious. Never more, I assured her. So she asked for proof in the form of an engagement ring. Not wanting to lose any momentum, the very next day I mailed her a cigar band from my best private stock.

It turned out that she was serious too, at least about the anniversary party so she came back down to go with me. Big tent, big crowd, big band, big supply of champagne, and one especially fun dancing partner. We happily partook to the full in everything that was offered. In the quiet times that followed we talked about how we had become pretty good friends over the years, and that might indeed be a reasonable foundation for a marriage, even though we weren't as young as we were, and even though statistically the odds were against it, for whatever that has to do with the price of beans.

So we traded in the cigar band for gold. And we traded in the single state for marriage. And Penny came back here after all. And we have become better friends than ever. We remember the day of our wedding with an ice bucket inscribed with LUGOT. "Let us grow old together." And that is what we have done over thirty-three years.

So whatever you may think of my sensible advice, my advice is: "Don't take it."

Wonderful Women

When I and my old friend Penny from decades ago and far away found ourselves married, we had a one-day hiatus from our six assembled children as a honeymoon. Later we decided to go on a more protracted version. We knew each other well from conversations over the years, but we wanted to deepen our understanding. So I took her to England to visit old haunts, old friends, my roots and what remained of my family in that heaven on earth.

It was important that the two women closest to me knew and liked each other. So our first visit was to my dear older sister, Pat, and her husband, Ian Mackenzie, in Kent. Ian met us at Heathrow and guided us on an extensive tour of the parking garage until he eventually found his car. He then navigated the motorways to the country lanes that took us to their home.

They lived in, and Pat still inhabits, a charming red brick and clay tiled Kentish farmhouse that they divided into two when their children grew away. One can see traces of its fourteenth century origins. The foundations are of clunch, a traditional building material in those parts comprising clay and chalk, and the half-timbered structure is in-filled with flint. Remnants of a minstrels' gallery are visible in the dining room. The functioning and equipment of heating and kitchen suggest that they are only barely newer. The oast house in the garden was once used to dry the hops that flavored bitter beer. All in all it was a perfect setting to introduce my American wife to my Merrie Olde.

As we crunched down their gravel drive, my beloved sister waved at us. She had that smile with the hint of mischief at the corners of her mouth that I remembered so well, but my antennae were out of practice. As was her wont, she took me by surprise. She greeted us with, "It's been a lovely year for rape!"

My wife was no innocent to be shocked by such language. But she was momentarily taken aback. Penny was at an unaccustomed loss for words. My sister relished jumping into the conversational gap with an explanation.

"It's been a wonderful crop. It looks as if the fields are covered in brilliant sunshine, a wonderful harvest for the rape seed oil." Aha, so that's what she meant.

We went inside the house, and I dragged our suitcases up the narrow stairs to our bedroom, where I gallantly chose the more uncomfortable bed, although it was a tossup.

Meanwhile, my wife had met my sister's "char", her long-serving cleaning lady, who was forlornly pushing an octogenarian vacuum cleaner around the cramped spaces between the over-crowded living room furniture. Tactfully, Penny observed that more dust was blowing out than was being sucked in.

"I know, dear," said my sister, "but she needs the money."

It was not as if much carpet was exposed since there was little floor space visible between the sofa, several chairs and stools, a desk, a chest of drawers, two bookcases, television set, radiogram, one grand piano, one upright piano and an organ. My sister and her husband were musical.

It did occur to my wife, who was observant if not preoccupied with fashionable taste, that interior decoration was not my sister's strong point. She felt it tactless to comment on the multiple colors and patterns of fabrics, cushions and curtains. However, she did ask why the area rugs surmounted four layers of fading and threadbare carpet that peeked from underneath.

"Well, dear," explained my sister quite unabashed, "we had a lot of old aunts, and when they left us their stuff we *couldn't* just get rid of it."

Talk of family continued when my sister recognized our late mother's heavy gold wedding ring my wife was now wearing, leading her to reminisce about the time that ring got buried when Mummy was kneading dough for saffron cake, a Cornish specialty. And she pointed out the scar in her skull where that ring had inflicted damage during one of her rare brushes with maternal discipline.

My brother-in-law arrived for lunch from his office in the converted oast house where he managed several agricultural estates.

He was enthusiastic about organic farming on a large scale and equally enthusiastic about his pre-prandial whistle wetter on a similar scale. Their drinks shelf was well and variously stocked from the mess of the Scots Guards, of which he was a retired officer. So we quickly prepared for an enjoyable interlude.

My sister provided a healthy lunch. We had offered to help get it, but there wasn't enough room in the kitchen. My brother-in-law needed a little help to finish the *Daily Telegraph* crossword. We were daily solvers of the *New York Times* puzzle and confident in our skill, but it proved that our transatlantic general knowledge was largely irrelevant, and we were out of tune with the multiple anagrams and puns. He quickly made up for it by regaling us with his own original puns, both sparked by the moment and drawn from a large store of memory.

Rolling her eyes my sister remarked, "It is such a change when we go on holiday to the continent. Then Ian makes puns in French."

After lunch Pat took us "swanning" through the Kentish countryside and to the Elizabethan red brick Sissinghurst Castle, the house and gardens having been lovingly restored by Sir Harold Nicholson and his wife Vita Sackville-West, members of London's famous literary Bloomsbury set. Vita was a devoted gardener and for years wrote a charming column for *The Observer*, one of Britain's premier Sunday newspapers.

We strolled through Yew Walk, past the Moon Gate, through the White Garden and around the orchard. The room in the tower was where Vita wrote her poems and novels and her charming and learned gardening articles. From the top of the tower the rolling countryside seemed illuminated by sunshine despite the overcast skies. It was an illusion, stemming from the fields of bright yellow rape.

Later, as we drove home past some woods my sister pointed out a hop field and said, "Look at that group of oast houses." This was the opening my wife was waiting for. She returned the service beautifully.

"I can't see the four oasts for the trees," she riposted with glee from the back seat. Her welcome into my family was swift and complete, and she and my sister have been the fastest of friends ever since.

Not that fondness inhibited my sister from the English sport of teasing "the Colonials" for their lack of culture and history or from her own appalling attempts to imitate an American accent. It did not take long for my wife to counter by protruding her front teeth over her lower lip and explaining in her equally appalling attempt at a British accent that, "The English have very bad bites and don't put braces on their teeth, so that's why they can't possibly help talking like this!" Try it.

The days were spent enjoying more treasures of the Kentish countryside, interspersed with ploughman's lunches at the charming country pubs: crusty bread with rich paté or Stilton cheese and pickled onions, washed down with the local draught beer. There were bucolic events like the point-to-point races sponsored by the local hunt, attended by more dogs than people, all of whom joined in the chase after the bookies trying to escape over the hedges with unpaid winnings while the last race was being run.

On Easter Sunday Penny and I drove to Canterbury, the seat of the Anglican Church, passing lines of pilgrims tramping across the Weald. We entered the cathedral founded by St. Augustine and saw the undercroft where the troublesome priest St. Thomas à Becket was murdered to please Henry II. We were quieted by the memorials to the warriors of centuries. We attended the magnificent morning service, sitting in the loft above the west end of the nave where, after the chanting of the psalms, the choir processed for the singing of the anthem, and the pure voices of the choirboys resonated through the high roof of the Norman sanctuary.

Penny and I visited great houses: Knole where Vita Sackville-West was born and grew up, where Virginia Woolf was inspired to write *Orlando*, and where the famous tasseled settees with their high sides furnish the state rooms. We went to Chertwell where Winston Churchill built his brick walls and painted, prepared his return to power, entertained his advisors, and occasionally relaxed during the war. He eventually gave the house to the nation for the recreation of his successors. We also visited the highly unusual fourteenth century fortified manor house, Ightham Mote.

Memories While Memory Lasts ❧ ❧ page 113

In the evenings our hosts shared their lives with us, much focused around the annual village shows based on Gilbert & Sullivan parodies for which for years they wrote, directed, cast, choreographed, arranged the music, promoted, and performed. When asked why they poured so much energy into this effort, my sister batted her eyelashes and replied, "It's the applause, dear." But all good things come to an end and the program notes for the final production read: "Mrs. Mackenzie will not perform her customary ballet solo this year due to advancing age."

Our visit to Pat and Ian came to an end as well. We headed towards our next destination and had to make a choice. Should we honor the invitation to go to Oxford for a degree day to collect my M.A. in person, all gowned, capped and hooded, or the other invitation to my old school in Bristol for a festive celebration at Clifton in a marquee on The Close? It was no contest. Feasting and dancing won over an academic Latin ceremony.

We headed west along the old main roads that offered a more intimate experience of the towns and villages than could the modern motorways. As we drove through Buckinghamshire I was surprised to see a sign to Shalstone, a village I had visited years before. We took the detour, passed near Stowe School (from which the actor David Niven was expelled for one too many mischievous pranks), past the turning to the famous Silverstone car-racing track and saw on our left the Biggin Hill airfield from which Spitfires defended the southeast of England during the Battle of Britain.

Turning into Shalstone we found ourselves on the ambitiously named Main Street with its handful of cottages and a church. I pulled up to speak to a shabbily clad gardener weeding shrubbery at the entrance to the manor drive. He asked me if he could help us. I said, "I'm Richard Hoskin. I'm looking for Geoffrey Purefoy."

"Richard!" he replied. "You're speaking to him!" Time had flown and we had lost touch, but it remains a small world. I asked if he would show my new wife his collection of old fashioned roses, and he treated us to a delightful stroll around the grounds. We chatted about old times and I asked after his former sister-in-law Shirley.

"As a matter of fact," he said, "I'll be going to her wedding in Somerset in a couple of weeks. She and Tony were divorced years ago." I asked him to give her my best wishes, said goodbye and we set off to continue our pilgrimage. I had last seen Tony on television at the Conservative party annual conference when he was chief agent.

I remembered meeting Shirley years ago at a Christmas dance that my housemaster at Clifton had arranged. He was enlightened as well as innovative and had encouraged us to go to dancing classes at the nearby girls' school. He probably thought this would divert our emerging hormones into healthy pursuits. So we had a good supply of dancing partners. At this dance I met the girl whom I later married and who became the mother of my children.

My study mate, Gorrie, brought a girl he had known when they had been evacuees during the war. (We wondered what would become of John Gorrie, and he delighted us when he became a successful actor and BBC television director, with major successes like *Edward VII* and *Lily Langtree* to his credit.) His dancing partner, Shirley, was only fourteen, but pretty and slender with auburn hair, wearing her first long dress, in pale blue taffeta. Above all, she was vivacious and spontaneous, loads of fun and was immediately popular.

After we all left school, she became part of the group that socialized together, going to the local hunt balls and various festivities. At a dance at the Pump Room in Bath, she was pursued by two would-be escorts, each trying to gain an advantage over the other. They were sitting out together on a settee with Shirley between them, both of them with an affectionate arm around her back. She got up to powder her nose. As she turned back she saw them disentangling themselves and blushing furiously as they realized that they were left amorously holding each other's hands.

The successful suitor was Tony Purefoy. After their wedding they spent their honeymoon in Innsbruck. When I married my high school sweetheart we sought their advice as to either Austria or Ibiza, then at its height as a fashionable island resort in the Mediterranean, and chose Innsbruck. Shirley and Tony later lived in the estate manager's house on the Shalstone estate, where my new wife and I visited them and had a marvelous time.

Tony and his elder brother Geoffrey were enterprising and energetically worked at making Shalstone a paying proposition. One of their projects was to fence pastures for sheep, including the rare

Jacobin breed. They were fortunate to employ an enormously strong former Polish resistance fighter who dug post-holes by hand at fantastic speed. A profitable sideline was selling large oil furnaces for taking the chill off country churches, a dire need.

Another project was to turn the stables into flats to rent out. Shirley delighted in telling the story of their tenant who was the glamorous French film star Brigitte Bardot, staying there while seeing a therapist to help her overcome her sexual inhibitions.

However, there was a cloud over this Eden. The brothers were childless. They were not surprised. The line had not produced male heirs for generations. A family legend tells of an ancestor, Admiral Purefoy, who had his wicked way with a gypsy's daughter, got her pregnant, and refused to recognize the child. Her furious mother placed a curse on the family, resulting in the lack of legitimate sons since. The solution was for the daughters to marry men who changed their names.

The spell was broken when Geoffrey's second child was a boy. Tony and Shirley followed with two daughters and two sons. James later overcame disappointment at leaving school early when he was not picked for the Rugby football team at Sherborne and expanded on his mother's enthusiasm for theater by becoming an actor himself. His movie roles have included the lead in *Beau Brummel*, Becky Sharp's husband Rawdon Crawley in *Vanity Fair*, and Mark Anthony in the television series *Rome*. His brother William Purefoy is an accomplished countertenor who has performed professionally all over the world.

A month or so after Penny and I got home I thought I would try to catch up with Shirley. After all, there is something irreplaceable about old friends. But she had moved and I no longer had her address. I relied on memory to address a letter to her in Martock, the village in Somerset where she had lived with Tony. It was a long shot that reached its target.

Some months later I got a reply. She cheerfully explained that she was no longer Shirley. She thought Shirley was a soppy name and much preferred her other name, Clare. That always brings to mind the translation in the Latin dictionary: *clarus, adj. clear, bright, famous.* Her surname had also changed with her new marriage to a retired Royal Navy fighter pilot. And she no longer lived in Martock.

Her new address followed the custom of the English post office of endowing a place with an address that was inversely proportionate to its size and importance. It included the name of the house, the name of the hamlet it was in, the name of the village the hamlet was near, the name of the small town the village was near, the name of the larger town the small town was near, and the county they were all in.

Nevertheless my letter with its sparse address had found her quite easily. It was thanks to the village postman, who had delivered her post before she moved. Like every man who had dealings with Shirley-Clare, he adored her. He put Shirley and Martock together and came up with Clare and Crewkerne.

Thus we reconnected, and I received a warm and amusing reply to my letter. Clare had built and sold a successful business, the Fosse Employment Bureau for clerical workers, but the buyer later dishonored the purchase contract. Bloody but unbowed, she invested the initial proceeds in holiday homes but ran into the collapse of the housing market.

When Penny and I were first on our way to visit Clare and her new husband Peter in their remote village, we got lost. Apparently Clare was clairvoyant and sent out her handyman (another of the men who would do anything for her) to find us. When we arrived at their ancient thatched house she was in full cry, with vivid accounts of organizing the village and patrolling the countryside.

The next morning she treated me with an enormous traditional English breakfast with bacon and eggs, sausages and kidneys, baked beans and fried bread. What bliss! Typically, thanking her for her characteristic kindnesses brought cheerful self-deprecation as she instructed me to, "Stop making such a bloody ridiculous fuss about bugger all!"

After breakfast, Clare roped me in with, "Hoskin, we're going cubbing," and hauled me off at high speed in her station wagon ("estate car" in English) through winding country lanes to follow the local fox hunt. The lack of success finding them brought redoubled efforts with higher speeds and more retracing of routes. Meanwhile,

Penny was privileged to be invited for a chat into Peter's private room that was usually dedicated exclusively to his reading *The Daily Telegraph* after his morning bath.

Through Clare I have reconnected with old school friends from Clifton and Sherborne. She organized a warm gathering of ten of us at the village pub, The Duke of Wellington, and her vivacity stimulated lively conversation. She regaled us with a childhood story of her evacuation to the country during the war. She told in convincing detail how she got off the train at the wrong station but was met by a childless couple who took her into their home, treated her with kindness and devotion and eventually adopted her.

Penny was at first fascinated by the story and then whispered some skepticism into Clare's ear. Clare chortled and whispered back that she had made the whole thing up to amuse us; in her own characteristic words it was "a lot of bloody codswallop!"

Clare became another of the special women in my life who have become good friends of my wife. We visited Clare and Peter during several visits to England but unfortunately they have been unable to return the visit to us. In part, their priority each year was driving across Europe in their camping van (deprecatingly called the "chip wagon") to their flat in Venice. But also a long flight was too uncomfortable.

Time had treated Clare's health unkindly, particularly with a disease London's best doctors could not diagnose that left her fragile and crippled. This culminated with a fall while we were staying with them. Peter suggested the pub for lunch. Clare and I walked slowly ahead, she riding her invalid chair and me walking alongside. As she got off the chair at the door to walk up the step I put my hand on her elbow when she suddenly collapsed, fell, and broke her wrist.

She had to stay in bed on the cold early morning we left, but nevertheless she came down in her dressing gown to see us off. Peter was still in his bath. Penny said, "You shouldn't have. We're quite capable of seeing ourselves off."

Clare exclaimed, "I wanted to make sure you didn't steal the bloody silver." She used her remaining energy to give us warm hugs and staggered back to bed.

Her poor health left her in her own words "absolutely knackered". But she dealt with this with the determination and good cheer that marked her overcoming other setbacks throughout her life. Her bodily energy was sapped, but her spirit and her kindness and vivacity remained unquenchable.

Clare and I remembered and celebrated many of our birthdays and sundry other occasions across the Atlantic, thanks to the miracle words and pictures of Skype, with joyful memories and lively conversations. But these dwindled. She was no longer fourteen. Though she has now left this earth, she will doubtless enliven many lives for long times to come. And I would not be surprised if one day she is helped up from her sofa in heaven, leaving her suitors holding hands behind her.

I Went Back

They say you cannot go back. But I do, every couple of years or so. The soil in which my roots were planted enriches me. It is partly about nostalgic memories, like going into a saddler's shop, inhaling the aroma of tanned leather, or maintaining membership in my London club. I keep my subscription to the National Trust and visit country houses and gardens, especially in my beloved native Cornwall. I choose to revisit the places that are still like they used to be. I also catch up with friends, especially old friends from those deeply fertilizing seasons of school and university.

Every time I spend a day or two in London, staying the night with John in Notting Hill Gate and Clive in the West End. They were old friends from school. Usually one's friends were in the same house. These were different. They were in my history class in the sixth form. We sat in the back row, Clive on my left and John on my right. It was not conscious but our seating reflected our politics. Clive was a socialist, I was a Liberal and John was a Conservative, although I was the only one who was rabid.

Our masters were marvelous and inspired us to be good historians, good enough to win university places. For Clive it was through elegance of style, for John through methodical application and for me through erratic but creative insight. Clive and I went up to Oxford where we got to know each other well, even though we were members of different colleges. John went to the other place.

Clive's avocation was journalism and publishing. He bought *Cherwell,* Oxford's weekly undergraduate magazine, where his style and modest but determined charm brought him success. My expectation was to make a career in another sort of journalism, following in my father's footsteps as editor of a weekly newspaper in Cornwall, *The Cornish Times.* To broaden my experience I pursued politics, Liberal politics in the English meaning of that misused word, following in the traditions of Gladstone, the Lords Russell and Palmerston, Asquith, the youthful Winston Churchill, Isaac Foot and his gifted sons, and the brilliant Jeremy Thorpe, my predecessor as president of the Oxford University Liberal Club.

Later Clive and my Conservative rival Michael Heseltine went into business together, and I wrote the foreword for their first publication. Michael was an effective debater and became president of the Oxford Union. He went on to parliament and came within a hair's breadth of achieving his youthful goal of becoming prime minister.

John predictably went into law and became a solicitor, later becoming a partner in the august London firm of Boosey & Co. that since the seventeenth century has represented the property interests of a farming family whose land was swallowed up by the growth of London. Lease-holding paid better than small-holding, and today the Dukes of Westminster and their Grosvenor Estate quietly manage major holdings in central London, San Francisco and Canada.

I spent the night before my first wedding in John's family house on the edge of Clifton Downs on the outskirts of Bristol, sleeplessly reading the *Book of Cricket* by Sir Pelham Warner, better known as "Plum". The next day John was an usher at my wedding. He later became godfather to my eldest daughter Sarah. (By the way, cricket was prominent in John's library. At school he established a record when he took ten wickets against Sherborne for 34 runs, an accomplishment akin to pitching a perfect game in baseball. Typical of his style, his game was steady and methodical.)

I much wanted Clive to be at the wedding, even though in those days it was "not done" for a Jew to participate in a Christian ceremony, but he was unable to make it. My first wife and I did spend the first night of our honeymoon in London at a hotel he recommended. Fortunately it was obscure enough to foil my loving sisters' efforts to cancel our reservation.

I kept in touch with John and Clive across many decades and thousands of miles after I crossed the Atlantic and permanently uprooted myself. They have both stayed with me in America. They each settled in London but saw nothing of each other after leaving school. Their only connection was through me. I visited them during my habitual pilgrimages to the ancient treasures of my homeland, until today I suppose we have become ancient ruins ourselves.

On a memorable visit a few years ago I stayed with John on my first night in London. He showed me the new pieces in his growing collection of eighteenth century Bristol porcelain. We reminisced about old school affairs and mutual friends. We had dinner at his local traditional Greek restaurant where John ordered in Greek and described another of his summers in Kos, his favorite island in the Aegean. He told me of his new interest in amateur athletics and his support for a woman Olympic middle distance runner.

The next morning we took our customary walk in one of the royal parks. John had become a parks commissioner and was unusually upset, as they had just gone through a trying experience. They had agreed to allow a trio of famous opera singers to put on a public performance. To their surprise and chagrin they attracted a vast crowd, more than the groundskeepers could handle. The concertgoers trampled the pristine grass and floricultural treasures and left huge quantities of litter. John regretted the commissioners' agreeableness and firmly stated that large concerts were simply not among the purposes for which the parks were lovingly maintained for public enjoyment. Never again!

The next night I stayed with Clive. I delved through new additions to his growing library, and we chatted about old school and university affairs and mutual friends. He told me about plans for new publishing ventures, including expansion overseas, in which he hoped I might join him. He suggested lunch the next day in his rather arty club since we had lunched in my club, the National Liberal Club near Old Scotland Yard the time before.

Over lunch I asked how his older brothers were doing. He described with enthusiasm how Neville was enjoying quite amazing success as an impresario. In fact, he had recently engaged The Three Tenors for a concert in an innovative venue that attracted an unexpectedly vast crowd, actually beyond their capacity to control. Nevertheless, Neville could not wait to mount an encore performance with an even bigger audience. He looked forward to staging it again in one of the royal parks.

They say you cannot go back, but I like to go back and I think "they" are mistaken. If I did not go back, how would my friends know what was going on?

Memories While Memory Lasts ❧ ❧ page 123

Passwords

One of the many challenges of striving for computer literacy at an advanced age is passwords. My computer tells me that I must protect my innermost thoughts and confidential figures and facts from not only the idly curious but also from those tempted to embark on a life of crime. Being of a law-abiding nature I always follow instructions. But coming up with enough passwords to protect the growing variety of my electronic activities is indeed a challenge to my imagination, not to mention my memory.

I have created ingenious passwords that nobody could guess, but later, neither could I. So I wrote them down on pieces of paper that I hid where no one would be able to find them. Unfortunately, neither could I. Now I have finally devised a solution. My companions in electronic striving tell me it is not original. They tell me that hackers could unmask my defenses. But it works for me. And above all it brings back memories, and anything that can do that is worth something.

I use the names of the dogs and cats that have graced my life. There is a drawback. When a beloved pet goes to that kennel in the sky I have to change my passwords. It is a bit of a nuisance, I suppose, but at least it provides practice in becoming ever more skillful in using my computer, and the demise of animals is infrequent.

Many of my pets preceded the computer age. That disqualified them because they were not trained in the requisite skills. It's amazing how many more technically adaptable puppies have been born in the present century compared with their predecessors. Thus I have not yet called upon the unfortunately ill-fated pets of my early childhood in Cornwall, but I do like to remember them.

Paddy was a smooth haired fox terrier. He was affectionate and playful with a fatal flaw. His hobby was worrying sheep. The local farmers complained, especially when their ewes miscarried. Paddy disappeared from our home. He was "sent to live in the country".

Passwords ❧ ❧ page 124

My ninth birthday present looked like a cocker spaniel from the front and a black Labrador from the back, pitching him at an awkward angle. I had been reading Rudyard Kipling's stories of India, so I called him Kim. I signed him up for the Tailwaggers Club. He proudly wore their medallion on his collar with his name and address on it. I trained him diligently, confident that in a matter of weeks he would be ready for a lucrative circus career. Over-confidence in his reliability to come and heel on command led to his demise. Someone left our front gate open, his curiosity overcame his immature discipline, and he ran into the road and was run over before my eyes. I still remember his lively ways on January 3rd every year.

I gave up on dogs for a while when the amazing Tigger came into my life. His story is told in *The Best Cat in the World*. He earned his stripes in multiple ways and was honored *post mortem* as my first password, but I am not going to tell you for what.

However, even amazing cats can't take the place of dogs, so I negotiated with my parents to have another puppy on condition that I regularly fed Tigger on my own for a whole month. I had already researched every possible breed and chose a Gordon Setter. I gave up on the circus and decided to become a crack shot and a famous quail hunter instead. The very next day our small Cornish town's weekly cattle market was held. Our fish monger Mr. Minards was at his usual pitch with an old baby carriage loaded with fresh fish brought up on the train from the nearby fishing port of Looe. I know I am repeating this story but I am telling it again because I enjoy it and hope you will too.

Mr. Minards had a cardboard box beside the pram with six adorable puppies tumbled up together on an old sack. They were not pure-bred Gordon Setters. My sister Pat said that they were probably pure-bred Black and White Cattle Dogs, a breed widely admired for their herding instincts. She thought they were known to be affectionate and playful, and could almost certainly be trained for practically any task.

She pointed out that Mr. Minards was asking only ten shillings each, which was quite reasonable for such a renowned breed. Her offer to finance the purchase immediately would allow me to repay her out of my pocket money over the next ten weeks. That would be much less expensive than a Gordon Setter and would not require saving up for weeks or a subsidy from my parents. The latter would certainly have brought conditions. Pat thought we could risk taking a pup home right away, and she practically guaranteed our parents wouldn't mind, much.

Confident that in a matter of weeks he would be ready to enter sheep dog trials, I could soon be famous as a world-renowned trainer and handler. The purchase was made. Holding my breath as we presented my choice to my mother, all she said was that she thought my puppy was adorable but needed a bath to get rid of his fleas and the smell that betrayed his farmyard origins. My father said I could keep him provided he didn't cry at night and keep him awake. My sister Pam said I should call him "Mack" after our Liberal parliamentary candidate John Mackintosh Foot, whom my parents greatly admired. She thought that would settle the matter, and she was right.

Mack's training began in earnest. His native instincts led him easily to his first task, which was to round Tigger up into a flock. The only drawback was that Tigger did not like being a flock and hissed at Mack and batted him on the muzzle with his sharp claws. I was confident that this could soon be overcome by training Tigger to cooperate, although my sister said any success with that experiment shouldn't lead me to training sheep in sheepdog trials.

Unfortunately, Mack was never to reach his world-beating potential. He soon caught distemper, a nasty disease for which there was no cure at that time. He died, and I was broken hearted. He has not yet made it as a password either.

I didn't feel up to the possibility of another canine heartbreak until I was married with a small daughter when we completed our household with a black Labrador. He came from a big country house and had quite a distinguished ancestry. We named him Rupert, which we felt was properly aristocratic. This deeply upset a childless couple who were friends of ours. Their puzzling rationale was that we should have guessed they had chosen Rupert for a boy if ever they had one. By then Rupert was reliably coming when he was called, and he clearly liked his name, so it stuck nevertheless.

Friends of mine had cheaply rented from the National Coal Board the shooting rights on thousands of acres of Northumberland moorland that had proved unpromising for mining. We all owned retrievers, and I was confident that Rupert could join the team as a well-trained black grouse retriever. We all planned on bringing home the bounty to our respective tables. Since I had a full-time job, I was realistic in limiting my expectations of devoting the time to train him as an international field-trial winner. Furthermore, when one grows up it is time to put aside childhood ambitions of world-beating fame in part time occupations. The occasional grouse would have to suffice.

The reason for the economical rent for the shooting rights became painfully clear. After hours of exhaustingly tramping through the heather in our shooting clothes one weekend after another, there was hardly a grouse to be seen, although on a memorable frigid Saturday we did see a lone bird hundreds of yards out of range. The moorland was as unproductive of game as it was of coal.

I had another friend, Tim, who successfully teamed up with his Labrador to bring teal and other duck to his table. Wildfowling required no shooting rights. One simply went to a place like the tidal marshes off Holy Island where duck and geese abounded. The only expense was a set of warm, waterproof clothes. The worse the weather, the better the sport. Tim chose nights when it was windy and rainy. He led me tramping across the mud flats on "splodgers", boards strapped to the bottoms of our waders to prevent sinking into the mud. We filled burlap sacks with hay, one for us and one for each dog. We carried them out to the middle of the marsh, where we lay on our backs on the sacks, trusting we had timed the tide movements correctly. We gazed shivering into the moonless sky and awaited our quarry.

Nothing happened. We waited, not that it was boring. True sportsmen are never bored. Then there were two gunshots and two splashes! On command Tim's Labrador brought each duck to his master. My Labrador Rupert did not think that was much fun. He seemed to complain about being cold and wet and not joining in. However, I caught on, and as my eyes grew accustomed to the darkness I made out the shadowy flights passing through the murk overhead. I shot my own gun and got quite near the target, hearing the pellets whistle towards the darkened moon. I could get enthusiastic about this, but Rupert would need more training to enjoy and meet the challenge.

Our opportunity was denied. I was sent to America. It was impractical to take Rupert, and anyway it was supposed to be for only two years. I left him with my boss who was a good friend and a sportsman. His sport was beagling. The beagles chased hares in circles and the men followed on foot. One had to call them "hounds". If one called them "dogs" it meant that you hadn't been beagling before. It was quite humane because the hares were in little danger. My boss was glad to have Rupert because he had recently taken up grouse shooting.

Rupert settled in very well. He enthusiastically took walks around the village making a lot of new friends. Soon a lot of new puppies appeared that looked like Labradors at the back and spaniels at the front, and even terriers, poodles and beagles at the front as well. Rupert never went wildfowling again. He didn't have time. He became well known. I *may* use him as a password, but I think I'll wait until his notoriety has been forgotten in that village.

Settling to life in America led to desire for another dog and a change of breed, while remaining loyal to my British roots. A friend of mine at the office, Gibby Carey, had a litter of English Setter puppies. Their dam was the outstanding bird dog Amy, who had been fired from her job with the Ohio Department of Wildlife. She had been hired out by the day to hunters visiting the state parks. The rangers ensured a good day's hunting for visitors by raising pheasants that they then drove out in their Jeeps to likely patches of cover early in the morning. They would tuck the birds' heads under their wings, rock them to sleep and hide them in the cover.

Amy was overqualified for her task. She had figured out that when the hunters took her out looking for game she simply had to track the telltale scent of Jeep tires. This led her unerringly to sleeping pheasants that she startled into flying into short range. Unfortunately, the hunters accounted for their allotted bags (the limit they were allowed to shoot) shortly after breakfast and complained bitterly to the rangers that their day of sport had been cut short. Amy was replaced by a less ingenious successor.

We bred a granddaughter to Amy. She was my son's dog, Bracken. He trained her diligently, and she became a wonderful bird dog. He followed an illustrated book that said that the best way to train a setting or pointing dog required a thousand acres. The second best way was with a pheasant's wing attached to a fishing rod, so being about nine hundred and ninety-nine acres short, that's the way he used. His puppy had a good nose and she got excited the instant she caught a whiff of pheasant. He got her chasing the wing in circles.

Then came the hard part, getting her steady on point. He tied a rope to her collar and looped it over the branch of a tree, holding the other end. With the rod in his other hand, he twitched it, moving the wing a few inches towards him. As Bracken rushed after the tantalizing wing he would jerk back on her leash and shout "Whoa!" Soon she learned this lesson: staying on point when the hunter flushed the bird and fired. He taught her with a cap gun and then a point two-two rifle firing blanks. Soon she was ready for a real hunt with live pheasants, *and* she was not gun shy.

Bracken was fast and covered a lot of ground. She proved to have an excellent nose, and she both found and tracked pheasant in cover with style and dash. One memorable fall morning she was tearing through the woods when she scented to her left. Bracken jammed on the brakes and held point with her body turned at a right angle!

However, she had two major faults. She would not go in water, and she was not interested in retrieving, striking a disdainful pose. Her body language said, "Retrieving is not part of my job description. I'm an expert in finding and pointing." One day we were out with my friend Charles and his German Short-Haired Pointer, Sarah. Bracken found a pheasant that I flushed and shot. Sarah retrieved it to her master's feet. Bracken was visibly seething and changing her mind about her job.

Moments later, Sarah found and her master flushed another pheasant which flew across in front of my son over the lake. Charles took the shot and the bird splashed down. Without hesitation Bracken swam out, retrieved it and deposited it at my son's feet! From then on, Bracken was an all around star.

Years later my fondness for choral singing led me to a friendship with Arthur, a tenor whose great enthusiasm was English Springer

Spaniels. He trained Springers. He shot over them; he handled them in field trials; he edited and published a magazine about them and he became nationally famous.

My wife Penny and I had been discussing completing our empty nest household with a dog but the debate about a suitable breed was inconclusive. I decided to take matters into my own hands. Her birthday was coming up. I planned on a surprise with my friend's help. I took her out for dinner at a restaurant north of the city. We were enjoying conversation and finishing our steaks when the waiter interrupted us with, "Madam, there is a phone call for you," and led the way to the coat room at the back of the dining room.

Around the corner stood my smiling friend, Arthur, holding a liver and white Springer Spaniel puppy in his arms, wearing a red ribbon around its neck. "Happy birthday, Penny!" Her response was succinct, "Oh, goodness!" But she didn't actually say "goodness".

We hastily finished dinner to the relief of the restaurant management, probably fearing a raid by the Department of Health, and hurried home. Penny quickly fell in love with the puppy and was playing with him on the living room carpet when she announced, "I'm going to call him Cedric." This was a suitable password, and I enthusiastically agreed.

I've written about Cedric, although not by name, in *The Lady and the Dog*. When he was still a small puppy Penny had to stay in bed for several days, and couldn't get up to let him out. He stayed by the bedside to look after her until I got home, and never once 'made a mistake' in the house.

He truly was a wonderful dog, intelligent, affectionate, eager to learn and biddable (up to a point). His webbed paws made him a natural in the water. His dam was a Canadian field trial champion and his sire Badger was from the famous Saighton strain in England and winner of the all-American high point field trial championship two years running. All this made him a wonderful finder and retriever of pheasants.

Now hunting pheasants was not quite what Penny had in mind when her birthday present arrived at the restaurant. But she was a good sport about it, especially when I allowed as how emeralds might indeed be more appropriate next year. The opportunity to serve roast pheasant to our guests outweighed any objections.

Cedric found living in the city a bit constricting, even though he went hunting most weekends and enjoyed lots of walks. We built him a cozy dog house at the end of a fenced-in run. He learned how to open the latch and let himself in when he wanted privacy. There were times when we didn't know what he really wanted, so we brought in an animal psychic to talk to him.

He told the psychic he was essentially happy, especially since we were not very firm with him, and he mostly got his own way. However, he confessed to destroying a major piece of furniture. It turned out he had scratched cotton stalactites in the undercover of our mattress, which wasn't so bad. He also had a friend, whom we hadn't known about, a neighboring Golden Retriever. The very next day this dog came to visit Cedric. They rubbed muzzles through the front gate. Fearful of the fast traffic at the end of the street, we let him in, and checking his collar for clues, called his owner. Meanwhile, the two friends spent the rest of the afternoon on our front porch deep in conversation.

Cedric turned out to have expensive tastes. What he really wanted was to live in the country with plenty of space to run and to have his own lake. So we moved to Kentucky, and found that we liked it too. He also loved summer vacations in Vermont where there was a bigger lake where he could swim all day long. It was there that he learned to dive. He was a prima donna, or perhaps a *primus dominus,* and enjoyed nothing better than performing for an audience. Over and over, he would run along the dock, dive on command into the lake like an Olympic racer, retrieve his dummy, and swim to shore amidst applause. He never tired of applause, reminding me of my sister Pat.

One evening the lake was deserted. I was reading on the dock, Cedric lying at my feet. Penny decided to go skinny dipping. She threw her bathing suit on to an overhanging branch and swam out to the rocks. She was just ready to come in when some neighbors launched their canoe along the shore. She called, "Richard, please bring me my swimsuit." Caringly I replied, "No," and went on reading, chuckling to myself. The neighbors paddled nearer.

Penny grew desperate. "Cedric," she pleaded, "Bring me my bathing suit, now!" He ran along the beach to the overhanging branch, reached up, grabbed her bathing suit in his mouth, and swam out to her with it. She put it on under water and swam modestly to shore.

Cedric shared our steak that evening. In fact, I observed his dinner was prepared much more lovingly than mine.

Unfortunately, Cedric was not immortal. We still miss him. He would be a hard character to replace. As I was used to the name Cedric, I had no difficulty remembering my password. We went for a whole year without a dog, convincing ourselves how convenient that was. But just as a theoretical exercise, after a few months we started discussing what breed we would choose *if* we were ever foolish enough to inconvenience ourselves with another dog.

I definitely wanted a real dog, not a convenient silly little dog that would be of no practical use. I preferred gun dogs for their intelligence and loyalty, and largely Penny agreed. Then we bit the bullet, or more likely the shotgun shell, and decided to go with the breed we had come to know and love and get another English Springer Spaniel.

One morning Penny went on the Internet to research a source. Her attention was drawn to an advertisement for puppies for sale not far away, Scotties, Aberdeen Terriers. Well, there'd be no harm in just looking, would there?

We were rational and concluded that two puppies would not be practical. So we agreed to take home the mother, just to see if we liked her. We were sorry for her too. She was only just over a year old, much too young to be bred. She had been kept all day long in a cage in a mobile home and didn't get much exercise. She was called Ebony because she was black. We thought that was a bit too cute, and Penny suggested we should call her Abigail instead, *if* we kept her. It sounded like Ebony but had more dignity. We did keep her, but she was a great disappointment.

When we got her home she went under our bed, and we hardly ever saw her. Everything was strange and frightening to her. She had never seen stairs before and had to be patiently taught to go up or down. Grass blowing in the wind startled her. Wild life scared her, even moths. We called the breeders to send her back. But they said she was truly outgoing and fun and we should persist. So we agreed, for a couple more weeks.

Abby told us she was always allowed to sleep on her breeders' bed, so we agreed just for a night or so until she settled in. We checked with them later and they told us she *never* slept in their room, let alone on their bed. By then it was too late.

We decided it was time for serious training to begin. Abby agreed. She explained her vocabulary to us, so that we could meet her needs efficiently. She acknowledged a few commands, but only for her convenience. "Come!" meant that she was ready to have us join her. "Sit!" meant that we should stop moving around. "Heel!" meant follow her at a respectful distance. A little grunt meant that she wanted to go outside. "Abby's chair!" means she can sit on our furniture wherever she chooses.

One term was new to us. She would clack her teeth in the evening to tell us it was time to go to bed. Then she would teach us new games with her favorite toys, like pushing "Gweek" off the bed for Penny to retrieve.

Pressing her forehead against mine at dawn meant that it was time for me to wake up and rub her tummy, and anything less than twenty minutes was unacceptable. Clacking teeth in the morning meant it was time for Penny to put her collar on and let her out for a bathroom run. If I picked up the collar she disappeared under the bed.

Glaring at us from under her eyebrows through the kitchen window meant she wanted to come in again. She expected her breakfast to be ready, but not to eat it until we were seated. We learned that breakfast was followed by a second run to inspect the environs and check that the wild life was behaving. This required loud fierce growls.

We were quick learners. We learned that she liked the ball thrown high so that she could catch it on the first bounce. She made clear that gardens were for digging in. After all, Aberdeen Terriers are earth dogs, and she was an expert.

Abby became outgoing and fun. She loves parties and doesn't wait for an invitation. She is a *smart* little dog. Don't let my friends who own real dogs know, but the fact is I became besotted with her. Keeping her meant that I had to change all of my passwords, but so be it. I won't have to change them again for a long time to come.

This all leads to the question, which breed of dog should we choose next? Do we want a real dog that is bred for a worthwhile purpose in life, like a gun dog or a herding dog? Or do we want a silly little dog that turns out to be cute, adorable, chatty and charming? Abby has asked for a pet, so we may have to decide soon. How about a West Highland Terrier? Bottom line, we must be practical about this. What password will our next dog produce? "Black & White" might be too easy to guess, but "Great Scotch" could be a puzzler.

I think I've got it. I've narrowed it down to five possibilities. For a hunting dog perhaps the German mouse hunter, the Affenpinscher or maybe the Tibetan boar hunter, the Kuvasz. If we got a pair I could use the plural in Tibetan, Kuvoszok. The Belgian Schipperke would be useful if we ever get a barge, not entirely out of the question. The Schipperke was bred to bark vigorously to repel boarders, to keep the barge free of vermin and to nip at the heels of the tow horses to keep them moving. Then again, I could branch into falconry and get a Hungarian Vizsla, or if we downsize our home with advancing age, a toy dog might be more practical, so perhaps we should choose a Chinese Shih Tzu.

Wait! Now I've really got it! Crossbreeds are all the rage. Even my sensible dog respecting son has got a Golden Doodle. I'll become world famous as a breeder of the new all purpose "Affenkuvaperkeviztzudoodle".

Unfortunately, there would be very little traffic on my exclusive membership web site for famous dog breeders, because nobody could figure out the password.

Teamwork

My wife Penny claims that the secret to the success of our marriage is a complete lack of communication. Now that might be more attributable both to her ability to look at things inside out and also to her original sense of humor, rather than, at least in my case, to the accuracy of her formidable powers of observation. But 'tis no matter. It is humor, originality and quirkiness that make her a continually refreshing and delightful companion. Accuracy is dull by comparison.

She exhibits an occasional inability to perceive my virtues as a housekeeper which, although admittedly subtle and erratic, are firmly based in good intentions. But she generously recognizes that I perform the less skilled tasks quite adequately from time to time. Of course, there is the possibility that neither of us is perfect. And there is the certainty that both of us would rather lead than follow. Where there's a will there's a stronger will. And so we have learned by osmosis alone, since verbal communication is out of the question, that often the best way to get things done is teamwork. We each do the part we do best while the other fills in the gaps. Penny claims I do my parts splendidly but points out the ever-widening dimensions of the gaps. In one instance, however, teamwork was definitely in play: the time I found a snake on our garden wall.

The wall in question is a retaining wall some eight feet tall, at our home in rural Kentucky, built of brick. I was puttering about the upper garden in the late spring doing some weeding when, being reasonably observant, I noticed a snake sunning itself on the top of the wall. It was very long and brownish-black with diamond markings, of a kind I had not seen before. I called Penny to come quickly and look. She was indoors working away and didn't particularly welcome being interrupted. But being a good sport she came out anyway, pronouncing with the confidence of one who had not seen it that I was making too much fuss about a common or garden snake.

Teamwork ~ ~ page 136

Then she saw it. It hissed at her and bared its fangs, showing the white interior of its gaping mouth. She yelled, "Watch out for that thing!" Then lack of communication took over and she rushed back into the house. I went discreetly back to my weeding a little further away. Then she came back with a new pronouncement.

"I've looked it up on the Internet. I recognize it. It's a Cottonmouth, a Water Moccasin. It probably came from our lake. It's dangerous. It's deadly poisonous. We must get rid of it. WE have got to kill it!"

With that she disappeared back into the house. That left me to deal with the snake. We had rapidly become a team of one.

Wearing a short-sleeved shirt and my snappy Smith & Hawken gardening shorts and carrying only a dandelion digger, I felt ill-armed to do battle with a deadly poisonous reptile. I went inside seeking reinforcements. However, the retreat had been strategic and my putative reinforcement was nowhere to be seen. So I settled for escalating my armed preparedness. I changed into a long-sleeved shirt and long pants that I tucked into my Wellington boots, picked up a pair of heavy-duty rubber gauntlets and headed out to the garage. There I grabbed a heavy metal rake and, now armed to its teeth and encouraged, I sallied forth to do battle.

However, the snake had disappeared. I was grateful that she whose admiration I cherished was not close enough to hear my sigh of relief. But my hunter's instincts had by now been fully engaged, and my eye caught the snake slithering into the corner of the courtyard. No excuses. Muttering a prayer of self-preservation, unconvincingly disguised as a tribute to my soon-to-be-fallen foe and keeping myself at a safe distance behind the long handle, I advanced with rake rampant.

I swung awkwardly, missing the evasive snake and hitting the concrete with a clang. Summoning up what residual coordination of hand and eye has survived with advancing age, I swung again. This time my aim was unerring, but ineffective. The tines precisely bracketed the snake's neck, chipping the concrete but leaving my enemy unscathed. My adaptive creativity kicked in, sparked by a finely tuned instinct for survival. I turned the head of the rake upside down. I swung again. This time there was a satisfying thunk and I prepared to declare victory. But the snake was merely angered. It writhed and hissed menacingly and gaped its jaws, displaying again its fangs and its cotton mouth. I swung again. Again it brandished its weaponry.

My emotions ran an unexpected gamut. The thrill of the chase ebbed, replaced by an admiration for a valiant foe and a reluctance to beat it into ignominious submission. This was not the hunt I was inured to, the sporting massacre of stupid pheasants, bred for sport and table and to be dispatched at a detached remove with a gentlemanly weapon. This was hand-to-hand combat. But how would I look as the doughty champion of my lady fair if I retreated from the lists and left my opponent to menace another day?

I steeled myself and followed the retreat of the rapidly slithering snake as fast as my awkward boots allowed. I swung the rake again and again. Many of the blows hit their mark. The snake's resistance dwindled with its movement. Finally it moved no more. There was no thrill of victory for me; just a sense of regret at the once living creature's agony of defeat in the one sided battle.

That evening over gin and tonics and enjoying the sunset on our porch, Penny and I celebrated, if not victory, at least freedom from fear. We had that afternoon invested in an anti-venom kit, and even read the instructions. We were now safer in the garden if not in the lake. However, with lightning quick thought processes only hours after the event, we connected the threat from the Water Moccasin with the danger posed by the occasional snapping turtle we had seen. Discretion took the better part of pleasure and we regretfully realized that our delightful excursions skinny-dipping in the lake had to come to an end.

But the story had not ended. The next day I decided to fork over my maturing compost heap. I was surprised to see just below the surface what I assumed to be domestic hen's eggs. But they were flatter than oval, and the shells were not as usual crushed for faster composting. I stuck the tines of my fork through the strangely soft shell of one. Inside was a baby snake! I dug deeper into the warm decomposing vegetation. Altogether, there were ten eggs, each with a baby snake inside. They were all dispatched to that snake nest in the sky.

Teamwork 〜 〜 page 138

I had verily saved my lady fair from large-scale danger, indeed a dire evil. Doing my best to temper any reprehensible hint of boastfulness, I communicated the significance of my conquest to her. Her relief was heartwarming. Imagine the joy in my triumph when she communicated to me her eternal gratitude, and told me that she always wanted me on her team.

Merrie Olde

I wasn't altogether sure about going back this time. The occasion, apart from the always-delightful prospect of visiting my perpetually youthful older sister Pat, was a school reunion. My wife and I don't do reunions, at least rarely, but this one promised to be different. It was unofficial and it was not organized by the school but my one of my contemporaries in my boarding house who persuaded a substantial group of us that if we wanted to catch up with each other while enough of us were alive, then we had better get on with it. Carpe diem before the days ran out.

His selection of invitees was based on those of us who had left school in 1950 plus or minus a year or so. He proffered a lunch at the school pavilion with the new headmaster, a rugger match, tours of the school buildings to see what had changed (including the Redgrave Theatre), tea with the current housemaster, an Advent carol service in the chapel, all climaxed by a grand banquet. The event promised maximum reminiscing with minimal pontificating.

There was another potential bonus. Our intrepid organizer was a glover, in fact he had been the Master of the Worshipful Company of Glovers. Founded when it separated from the much older Cordwainers in 1349, it lives by the motto of *"True hearts and warm Hands"* and retains the privilege of presenting the sovereign with a gift of gloves on the occasion of the coronation. He thought it might be possible to introduce me to membership. This brought with it the added privileges of the London livery companies, conditional only upon swearing loyalty to the Lord Mayor and paying "quarterage". One could drive one's flock of sheep across London Bridge without let or hindrance. And one was permitted to relieve oneself against the wheel of one's vehicle in public. However, Hertz was unlikely to be familiar with this provision.

There was a drawback. Following the reprehensible modern British habit of imitating many American customs, and being influenced by the popular media to follow the worst while being unaware of the best, our good organizer decided to include wives. Now I knew only one of the wives, and my wife knew none of the men, so the conversation would in all likelihood be diverted from what interested us enough to attend a reunion, in other words reconnecting with close friends from our boyhood who had largely not seen each other for fifty-eight years. But at least we could rely on them all to have retained the British characteristic of self-effacement so that we would not be subjected to boasting about personal success and exceptionally gifted and talented offspring.

My ever-resourceful wife suggested that I replace her by taking as my guest an old friend Clare, who knew and was popular with many of us. It was a good idea but impractical because Clare's health was not good, a reminder that if we wanted a reunion we had better get on with it. So get on with it we did, and we went.

It turned out to be the best visit ever. The reunion was the highlight. There were many other memorable times, including visits to the dwindling population of old (and getting older) friends, to familiar places, and the food. Ah, the food!

To put it into objective context, the reunion did summon memories of school food. The war had brought about a change from eating in houses to the entire school eating centrally. There were excuses, given post-war shortages and rationing. But it was not a cherished gourmet experience, and both the menu choices and the influence of public opinion were limited. Horse appeared only briefly on the menu, since even hungry British boys vociferously lacked the sweet tooth of carnivorous Belgians or Frenchmen. But whale and powdered mashed potatoes showed up predictably on Mondays. Even describing the gelatinous lumps as "steak" did little to assuage the taste buds, let alone the extremely challenged mandibles of the ravenous young.

Fortunately for me, there was a rare but welcome alternative. Tripe and onions. Since there was no competition, I could get a second helping. Delicious! I had acquired the taste for the more exotic offerings of the British table from my mother, who not only rose to but also clearly enjoyed the challenges of feeding a family during wartime. So my family was nourished not only by the two ounces each of beef and mutton per week (at least enough to make

Cornish pasties), but also by the tasty delights of wild rabbit stew, rare liver and onions, calf's brains on toast, beef's heart with suet and home-grown sage stuffing, steak and kidney pie (although I preferred the steamed suet pudding version), mince pies with goose fat pastry, and chicken liver paté.

Excuses for poor food extended to British restaurants, which emphasized filling starches, made a virtue out of self-sacrifice, and considered discernment about taste as Frenchified, effete, and un-British. The Common Market has changed all that, and the tastes of the more prosperous population demand better from the fancy restaurant to the local pub alike.

Penny and I did not plan our trip around gourmet experiences, but the excellence of the food found us wherever we went. When we weren't in people's homes, we simply made a beeline for a pub where the traditional picturesqueness of the thatch was an indicator of the charm of the interior and the tastiness of the food. At the seventeenth century New Inn in Rye in Sussex we had our first of many steak and kidney puddings, with chips and mushy peas, washed down with the local bitter and a dry Smithwick cider. The savory gravy had soaked just enough into the suet crust to score high on the nostalgia quotient.

At the Six Bells near Petworth in West Sussex we ate rare liver and onions by a log fire in the snug, followed by an excessive treacle pudding. At The George near West Meon in Hampshire we enjoyed a ploughman's lunch with a chunk of cheddar, crusty local bread and homemade paté. By the time we reached Middle Chinnock in Somerset, the irrepressible Clare had organized a table for eight of us at The Lord Nelson, where the local brew did not fit into half-pint pots, the local ham was succulent, and the good cheer abounded.

On to Torquay lying beneath the red cliffs of Devon and to the fish and chip shop on the seafront facing the Channel. Simple food, a delicious lightly battered fried fresh-caught plaice with the chips dowsed in malt vinegar. Neptune's feast, so good that we asked the landlord's wife at the little pub in Bath around the corner from our bed and breakfast to cook it for us again. That was a wonderfully sociable evening where we were welcomed by the cheerful habitués around the bar, from the old Scot in the threadbare overcoat enjoying his weekly pint to the racehorse owner back from a meeting in

America, the feisty grandmother known fondly to all as "The Dragon", the young couple who socialized mainly with themselves, and the chap from the neighborhood who chatted up my wife. "My husband's from Cornwall," she pronounced as she established rapport. "Well, I don't suppose you can hold that against him," was the response.

Undaunted, Penny accompanied me to Cornwall where we based ourselves at a small private hotel between Liskeard and Looe, converted from the home of a wool merchant. It was run by an enterprising couple with a gift for the trade they had taken up after he had retired as an inspector with the Metropolitan police. As a young man in the RAF he had been a chef at a base that entertained distinguished guests. His culinary skills and repertoire were impressive. He asked that one order dinner from the menu during the afternoon. After wrestling with choices, each sounding more delicious than another, we settled for the best dinner of our visit, rare roast rack of English lamb with mint sauce, roast potatoes, parsnips, carrots and peas, divinely prepared and presented.

And one must not forget the Cornish pasties that we bought in little shops on the road, with such a choice of ingredients baked inside the pastry case that the devil avoided Cornwall in fear that he might end up inside one. Now we never did see a Starry Gazey pie with the pilchards' heads peeping out from the crust, and it was not the right season for ice cream made with Cornish cream. Nor can we overlook the "full English breakfast" which we must have enjoyed a score of times, fried lean bacon, bangers, fried eggs, tomatoes, mushrooms, baked beans and the irresistible fried bread. Heaven on earth on a daily basis!

I must make a quick detour before sharing the banquet at the school reunion. In London we of course partook of more steak and kidney pie at the pub along from the Victoria & Albert Museum. But above all we went through the food hall at Harrods and then spent most of a morning drooling through Fortnum & Mason. The food is mouth watering. The fish: smoked haddock, Craster kippers, smoked trout, eel. The meats: York hams, brisket. The game: pheasant, grouse, quail, jugged hare. The delicacies: quail's eggs, country paté. Cold-water crust pies of all kinds—veal, ham and egg; game; bacon, hard-boiled egg and chipples. And the bakery: farmhouse loaves, round loaves, baguettes, Eccles cakes, confections.

We come now to the banquet in its magnificent setting. One of our contemporaries (who had been in the wine business) was a recent master of the Society of Merchant Venturers of Bristol, and his younger brother was the current Master. The society had started life as a merchant guild, and had backed John Cabot's voyage of discovery to Newfoundland in 1497. Over the centuries they had made fortunes in the slave trade. Street names in Bristol are a reminder, Whiteladies Road, Black Boy Hill, Jamaica Street. But these days the Merchants focus on charitable endeavors, supporting education in particular. Their guildhall includes a banqueting room with elegant furniture, silver, china, paintings, and fabrics, topped off with magnificent service.

The menu was worthy of the setting and enhanced the occasion. As we all gathered with our wives, we enjoyed a champagne Duval Leroy. The first course was a wild Loch Fyne smoked salmon (entirely superior to its farmed relation offered by super markets), accompanied by a 2007 dry Macon Chardonnay Cuvee Joseph Talmard, a taste whetter to linger over. The entrée was roast pheasant with roast potatoes, parsnips and curly kale. What a delight to be presented with parsnips without needing a special request! The wine was a 2004 vintage from the Chateau Emilion, a perfect complement to the rich game flavor: Chateau Franc Baudron Montagne. Dessert was a traditional bread and butter pudding, a peasant favorite. The whole feast was capped with excellent brandy and liqueurs with our coffee, sipped as we enjoyed the elegant and amusing toasts and speeches.

And so a brief visit to a nephew in London and thence to the airport and home. But we took more gustatory experiences with us at the last minute. Heathrow airport has a food shop. We stocked up with a whole smoked salmon, crocks of paté, smoked lean bacon, a whole Stilton cheese, and a packet of chocolate digestive biscuits, a bag full of nostalgia. Of course Britain is not like it used to be. Would I go back again? Would I risk disappointment? I cannot wait.

Jailbird

To keep your spirits up in dire situations you have to see the funny side. Alone and despondent and looking around my jail cell to scope out my surroundings I spied a message and a drawing scratched in the chipped dark green paint on the wall beside the barred and bolted door. The message read:

Today my heart is full of joy
Cos' I got here before Kilroy.

The drawing was of the cartoon character that was all the rage in the early sixties, domed head, long nose, hands gripping the top of a wall that he was peering over.

That cheered me up and encouraged me to get out of jail before Kilroy came visiting. I comforted myself that at least this was one weird situation in which my Procter & Gamble carpool friend Gibby Carey was not involved. Gibby is a gifted raconteur who amuses his companions with a limitless repertoire of unique characters he has met and improbable situations in which he has participated, from sponsoring a traveling circus to my favorite, the time when he was at a party in Maryland gathered around the swimming pool at the home of Allen Dulles, head of the Central Intelligence Agency.

Mr. Dulles was overweeningly proud of his prize bull and ordered it to be led out and shown off to his guests. Unfortunately, the surround to the pool had been splashed by divers and was slippery. As the bull rounded the corner with more enthusiasm than agility, he lost his footing and fell into the deep end.

Guests were splashed and discombobulated, and the bull thrashed about trying to clamber out. Flustered efforts by the bull's keeper to pull him out only increased the drenching. Gibby was there to come to the rescue. He called for the farm's front-end loader and found stout canvas straps used for lifting heavy barrels.

Gibby asked the guests to move away from the shallow end, a suggestion followed with alacrity. The keeper led the bull from the deep end, swimming and eventually walking, down to the shallow end. A farm worker positioned the front-end loader and the bull's keeper placed the straps around his charge's belly. After much squirming and kicking the bull was elevated to dry land and led to his pen bellowing indignation. The guests resumed their party. There was no small talk. What a story! Well, at least Gibby was not involved in my present adventure. It would be my story to tell.

The tale begins with my return from England to Cincinnati to set up expanding the American exports of a British concrete machinery manufacturing company based in Newcastle upon Tyne, run by a friend of mine, Kenneth. First thing I needed was a car and I bought an almost new station wagon from a man being transferred overseas.

We agreed to meet at the car rental agency on West Sixth Street in Cincinnati where I would return the car I had rented for the past week or so. I stopped at a traffic light, checked the rear view mirror and saw the flashing red light of a police cruiser. I pulled over. The driver got out, put on his cap, walked to my car and motioned me to wind down my window.

"What's your name?" I told him. Then he said, "You are under arrest."

"What??? What for?"

"Stealing a rented car."

"But I'm on my way to return it. It's just a couple of blocks ahead."

"That's what they all say. Get out of the car, and keep your hands in plain view."

I obeyed as another uniformed policeman with a companion wearing a raincoat and, yes, a snapped brim Fedora appeared on the sidewalk. "You're coming with us," the man in uniform said, unsnapping handcuffs from his belt.

"Wait a minute," I protested, "there's been a mistake." I told him my story. He seemed convinced when I asserted that I was meeting the seller to pick up my new car at the rental agency in a few minutes. He whispered to his companion, who turned out to be a detective.

"Okay, but you'll have to tell that to the judge in the morning. We just follow orders. We'll take you to our car. Walk between us." The detective put his courteous but firm hand on my elbow.

"Where are we going?"

"City jail."

"Good grief!" I said, or words to that effect.

"But I've got to let the guy who sold me his car know. He's expecting me at the rental place."

"We'll let him know," the detective said and got on his radio. "Good news," he reported. "He said he'll show up in court tomorrow as a character witness."

We wove through rush hour traffic with me caged alone in the back seat. When we reached City Hall, great double doors opened to allow us entry to the bowels of the building. *"The dungeons,"* I thought and was not far wrong. They escorted me into a dingy building peopled by uniformed men at untidy desks interviewing gloomy ill-dressed committers of unknown crimes. The place smelled of stale urine exaggerated by disinfectant.

My captors turned me over to a jailer, gave him some details to enter in the form on his desk, wished me luck and left to join the hunt again. The jailer instructed me to leave my raincoat, jacket, wallet, watch and belt with him and filled out a receipt. "But my trousers . . ."

"We don't want you to hang yourself," he explained. "You can make one phone call."

I called the people where I was staying. We had become good friends with John and Cookie and their family, and John and I were godfathers of each other's sons. When they had heard I was back in Cincinnati, they hospitably invited me to leave the Mariemont Inn and stay with them at their new home, which I had gratefully accepted.

I told them my story, and John enthusiastically assured me he would get right on it, post bail and enable me to sleep in comfort at their house before going back to City Hall for the court hearing in the morning. He would also call a mutual attorney friend and ask him to plead my case to the judge. I gave John the number to call at City Hall to arrange bail. Such a relief.

I went back to look for other messages on the walls of my dim cell and await rescue. The jailer came to my cell again and unlocked the heavy door. "You've got a phone call." It was John.

"I couldn't arrange bail. I was told I could use the bill for our real estate tax to show we were responsible, but we've only just moved into the house, and there is no record of our having paid. They won't accept a check or a credit card. I don't have enough cash lying around, and bailsmen are expensive. Doesn't seem right. But I talked to an attorney friend and he will come to court tomorrow to represent you. We'll meet him first thing."

"You mean I'll have to stay in this stinking black hole all night? Isn't there anyone you could borrow the cash from?"

"I've got an idea," said John. "I'll call Gibby. He always thinks of something," and hung up.

"Good grief," I thought. "I suppose that was inevitable, but at least Gibby is good at getting things out of the deep end."

As I waited hopefully for another call and late afternoon turned into evening, the cells nearby filled up with more sorry characters, many obviously drunk, some with three crowded into one cell. I was privileged to have the Kilroy cell to myself. Time passed.

The jailer reappeared. "Come and collect your things. A guy is here to pick you up. He's posted bail. Be sure you're back early in the morning."

John was waiting in the now crowded office, smiling.

"How did you pull this off?" I asked.

"It was Gibby Carey," John chortled. "He buys his gas from a guy in Terrace Park, knows him well. He's always got plenty of cash around, was glad to lend it to Gib. You're free, for now," and drove me home complete with wallet and belt.

At the crack of dawn John drove me downtown to the City Hall. I thanked him for taking me, otherwise I would have had to take the bus and walked. "Wouldn't miss this for the world," he said.

We found our way to the appointed municipal courtroom, already crowded and humming with anxious whispered questions and reassurances. My attorney spotted us and beckoned us over.

"I tried reasoning with the rental agent to drop the case but he was adamant. He said he had cars stolen recently by people giving fake addresses and absconding and needed to make a statement. At least I know the judge and was able to have a word with him, but this could get serious. He promised to put us on early. I'll do what I can."

The car seller was seated at a bench, good as his word. John and I joined him, and the proceedings began. The judge was no nonsense. There was a lengthy docket. The first case was a demure and conservatively dressed little old lady. The bailiff's whisper was audible all over the room. "Shoplifting, your honor, fifth offence."

The old lady did not have an attorney. She tried to plead her case. The judge was impatient and decisive. "Authoritarian," whispered John.

"But your honor, I only picked it up to have a good look."

"Ninety days," said the judge. "Take her down."

"Next case," announced the bailiff. "Stolen rental car." He called the rental agent, who looked sleazy but triumphant.

"This guy acted suspicious. He didn't have a credit card for a start. He paid the deposit with cash. He gave his address as the Mariemont Inn and said he would return the car within a week. And he had an English accent. When he never showed up we called the Inn, and he had checked out early. He left no forwarding address, some story about staying with friends in a new house he didn't have the address for."

My attorney addressed the judge. "This is completely ridiculous," he began. The judge interrupted. "Case dismissed." He banged his gavel. The rental agent looked furious and then foolish. We all smiled and left immediately taking my attorney with us for a brief celebration.

And so justice was done. My friendly attorney was a star. My newly adopted country showed its stripes as a haven of democracy. But did those poor people in the jail and in the courtroom get justice or mercy? None of them were wearing business suits. Did they have friends to call to help them out? Did they know attorneys with influence and connections that carried more weight than legal arguments to get them out of jail?

And what if I had newly arrived to carry out my business mission? What if I had no personal connections? How long before I could have got a credit card if my record had been blotted with a jail term for theft?

Well, ever since that experience, I have used a credit card to rent a car and I have carefully read every clause and filled out every space in the rental agreement before driving off with their car. I have let them know if I needed to keep it longer than expected.

And I am not among those who clamor for law and order or demand "three strikes and you're out". I certainly believe in the rule of law, but I urge that justice be blind, thorough, fair and merciful. I have not raised my voice as loudly as I should, but I fervently hope that those responsible for leading this great country are wise in their views and balanced in their practices regarding the just administration of justice.

There is a footnote; it is new. After many years, I ran into Gibby just the other day and we reminisced about this story. He said, "No, I didn't get the money from the man at the gas station. It was a challenge to get it together; none of us had that much cash lying around. I rummaged around Cookie's girdle drawer and found her secret stash. That's where it came from!"

Heavens, is my memory not what it used to be? Or perhaps Gibby is misremembering. But I remember what John told me. Gibby remembers what he did. Either way, it is time to get my memoirs written down.

Spring Cleaning

Snowdrops boldly led the way, followed by the more timorous and showier crocuses. Relief for cabin fever was in the air. I seized the moment for weeding and raking of left over leaves.

High powered thorough house cleaning took over to ensure that everything was spic and span for the return of our cleaning lady from wintering in her condominium in Florida.

One precious item that was brought into the light of day and hung outdoors from a branch of our Bradford pear to air out was my father's Crombie overcoat. This amazing coat was powerful as a functional garment. It was made in Scotland to fend off the penetrating damp cold of highland winters. Its outer parts were of thick cut pile wool, with a quilted lining. The only time I ever felt less than toasty in it was walking along Lakeshore Drive as wind knifed across a frozen Lake Michigan into the heart of downtown Chicago.

Its weight provided another special bonus. Many was the dining occasion that I delighted in the startled expression on the face of a courteous *maitre d'hotel* as he helped me into it, staggering under the unexpected weight.

The Crombie was also a powerful emotional tie. My father gave it to me when I left my home in balmy Cornwall for the tundra in Northumberland, where nor'easters howled in from the North Sea. It was his favorite overcoat. Giving it to me was typical of him. He literally offered me the shirts off his back, but they did not fit.

I have carried that Crombie with me to and fro' across oceans and continents for over fifty years. It was my favorite overcoat too. But in recent years it has lived mostly in the spare closet upstairs. I have to admit it has been unfashionable for at least forty years, never a concern of mine. It is also true that modern materials offer equal warmth with lightness and convenience. But I couldn't bear to throw it out. It was a memento.

Then spring cleaning came. The coat had some bits of fluff on it. So I took it outside to brush it off, and hang it on the branch to air.

Spring Cleaning ~ ~ page 152

The reality became apparent in the sunlight. It was hopelessly shabby. I applied the ultimate test. If I offered it to my son to wear in the Colorado winters would he accept it? After all, he has a strong sense of heritage and family tradition. I did not have to ask him to know his answer. No way. Goodwill wouldn't take it for sure. My heart was heavy as I contemplated the choices that lay ahead.

 I threw the Crombie out. I felt I was breaking a connection to my father. Quickly, however, I realized that what I was discarding was a clumsy and inconvenient object that had no further function. The memories remain, robust and warm. There is a little more room in the spare closet for what I may actually wear in the next couple of years. I reluctantly realized that my spring cleaning has not been completed. I am still an inveterate hoarder of mementos. But I do feel a little more room to open up to the rebirth that springtime brings.

Wimbledon

The weather in England is always officially perfect in the last week of June and into early July. That is because it is Wimbledon fortnight. And when one plays tennis on grass courts (used at other times for intensely competitive croquet matches), not like those horrid artificial modern surfaces, the weather must cooperate.

I played tennis at school, largely because I was not much good at cricket. I lacked superlative coordination of hand and eye. My highest score as a batsman was 23 not out, and my slow bowling was an invitation to mayhem. I did manage to be selected to represent School House in the tennis matches, playing for the third pair with a devastating game at the net compensating for my proclivity for double faults when serving.

My study mate Paul Sochor was a star, not only at tennis but also squash, racquets and cricket, representing the school at any sport involving a ball and an implement to hit it with. His parents had fled Czechoslovakia after the rise of Hitler and got into manufacturing printed fabrics in Belfast. His mother had risen to become Czech national women's tennis champion on the strength of her backhand. Paul evidently inherited his mother's genes, and by the time he arrived at Clifton at the age of thirteen, he was junior tennis champion of Northern Ireland.

Incidentally, I had a business trip to Belfast a few years later and visited Paul. He had plenty of time on his hands, because my visit coincided with an official state visitation by the Queen Mother. The police took the precaution of locking up the known republican troublemakers for the duration. Several workers at the Belfast Silk & Rayon Company were among them, so the factory simply closed down for a few days.

Anyroad, the summer we left school Paul played in the West of England tennis tournament in Bristol and roped me into umpiring. We got to know several players including the Czech lefthander,

Jaroslav Drobny, who was fancied to win Wimbledon that year. He and Paul conversed fluently in their native tongue while I listened in awe.

Tennis was still an amateur sport in those days, and the players were an interesting international set, all dressed on the court in impeccable white. I got to know a delightful chap called Nobby Clark. He was from Bristol and had been an executive in the Anglo Iranian Oil Company. Nobby made a lot of money on the side in partnership with the Shah importing large second-hand American cars for use as taxis in Tehran. Only an average tennis player, he somehow wangled a place as a member of the Persian Lawn Tennis Association official delegation. Nobby arranged for me to become a member too and invited me to join him at Wimbledon where we sat in the competitors' gallery on Centre Court. This was above the baseline at one end of the court opposite the royal box.

Nobby arranged for me to stay in London at the very tony Dolphin Square where he had a flat. It was also the location of the Rockingham Club, which I had never heard of but soon learned more about than most young men from rustic Cornwall.

At Wimbledon we came and went as the whim took us. Once I found myself sitting next to Frank Sedgman, one of the talented Australians who dominated tennis in that era, along with the likes of Ken McGregor, Ken Rosewall, Roy Emerson and Rod Laver (whose left forearm was almost twice the size of his right). It should have been a glamorous star-studded moment, but Sedgman's pervasive halitosis forced me to move into the row behind him and sit next to a non-athletic fellow who turned out to be David Tomlin, star of the light comedy film *The Little Hut*, no tennis star but very jolly. He later had a role in *Mary Poppins*.

Drobny was seeded second and playing well in the third round against Britain's Tony Mottram, but when his girlfriend showed up during the second set, he lost his concentration and the match. It was the American Dick Savitt who possessed the fortitude to maintain his form throughout the tournament and went on to become the gentlemen's singles champion.

I found the tennis fascinating, but it dawned on me that Nobby Clark was more interested in the players than the play. He particularly focused on Keith, an extraordinarily handsome young South African who had been part of our group in Bristol. As it turned out Keith was staying at Dolphin Square too, also in a room arranged by Nobby.

We spent the evenings in the Rockingham Club, stylishly furnished and decorated, with a white grand piano at which a handsome dark man played sophisticated standards. The Mexican ambassador was there late every evening looking rather dissolute and staying to the end. Nobby said he drank two bottles of gin every day. Apparently every afternoon he had his chauffeur drive him from the embassy into the country to spend time with sheep, to whom he was very attached. Nobby encouraged me to acquire a taste for gin and tonic, served in the authentic British fashion without ice, allowing the flavor and aroma to come through.

Being observant, I noticed by the third evening that all the club staff and patrons were men; no women to be seen unlike village pubs in Cornwall. Light was shed on this by a middle-of-the-night phone call to my room. Keith, the handsome South African player, was distraught, in tears. He demanded to know where Nobby was. He had seen him leave the club with an attractive young man, and he had not come back. It dawned on me that Keith was in love and needed comforting, hinting that perhaps I would welcome him to my room. I told him I had to go back to sleep and might see him at breakfast.

When I caught up with Nobby in the morning he was uncharacteristically irritated and seemed to be thinking that Keith was not such a great idea. I must say that Nobby always behaved like a perfect gentleman with me and I continued to enjoy his friendship from time to time that summer after getting back to Bristol.

Nowadays whenever I watch Wimbledon on television I feel nostalgic for the much more vivid and intimate view I once had in the competitors' box. But whatever the venue, an unmistakable tickle of gin and tonic tantalizes my nostrils.

Star

We new immigrants to Cincinnati used to say (flattering ourselves that we were original when we first said it) that this was a good city to live in because it was big enough to host major civic institutions and small enough to welcome fresh participants into its civic and social lives. It was true.

The institutions included not only successful professional baseball and basketball teams but also excellent cultural organizations, including a major art museum, first class symphony orchestra, renowned annual choral music festival in May, improving opera, and recently founded professional theatre and ballet companies. These institutions, added to a well-earned reputation for vision and integrity in local government, were the cultural backdrop to a self-confident sense of civic pride.

We were welcomed into the ranks of volunteers who provided effective support to the arts. We served on boards of directors and on energetic men's and women's committees that raised funds and created audience-building events. All this vitality attracted world-class directors and performers who enhanced the product offered to the ticket buying public.

My English wife and I were particularly interested in the Cincinnati Ballet and were invited to join its board. The company was closely connected with the College Conservatory of Music at the University of Cincinnati, and in the mid-sixties it hired as director David McLain, the head of the college's dance division, together with a core group of ten professional dancers. A year or two later Carmen DeLeone was brought in as music director and conducted an orchestra drawn from the Cincinnati Symphony in increasingly polished performances.

In the early sixties the great British dancer Alicia Markova retired from performing but did not end her career. She taught ballet and inculcated her love and enthusiasm for classical dance in young dancers. Markova was born Lilian Alice Marks in Finsbury Park, a not very fashionable part of London. She was a frail child. The family doctor recommended that she be given lessons in what was then called "fancy dancing" to strengthen her legs.

Her grace and talent, not only for dance but also for performance, bloomed and soon she was performing as "The Child Pavlova". As she grew in skill and maturity her teacher introduced her to Diaghilev, who was so impressed that he invited her at the age of fourteen to join his company in Monte Carlo and renamed her to appeal to the Russian taste of international ballet aficionados.

I do not know this as a fact, but I speculate that this is where Markova's connection to Cincinnati had its roots. In the mid-thirties, the temperamental quarrels that mar artistic endeavors divided the company. One half became the Ballet Russe de Monte Carlo backed by a new company, World Art, Inc., formed to bring ballet to America. World Art was founded by the Cincinnati philanthropist Julius Fleischmann, whose grandfather had made a fortune in yeast and gin.

"Junkie" Fleischmann was a passionate lover of the arts; he even named his yacht "Camargo" after the great dancer. He was also a world traveler and amassed a collection of paintings during his travels in Europe. Today I enjoy two of those works by the Italian artist Franzoni.

The British government regarded Markova as a national treasure. During the war she was protected by being sent to America. She starred with the Ballet Russe de Monte Carlo and later with the American Ballet Company and toured with a troupe presented by the impresario Sol Hurok. During that time she danced throughout the Americas. She told me of a vivid memory of Argentina where the president dictated that she dance for Eva Peròn, "The Lady".

She loved to tell the story of an experience while performing in Mexico when she rested for a few days in a fishing village on the Pacific coast. A village elder sought her out and offered to sell her the village for £5,000. That would take much of her savings and be hard to get out of Britain during that time, and anyway her interest lay in dance not in foreign real estate investments. With that little twitch at the corners of her mouth that I grew to know well she said, "So I passed on the opportunity to own Acapulco."

Another immigrant who enlivened the Cincinnati ballet scene at that time was P. W. Manchester. Also born in London, "Bill" Manchester was a devoted fan of two arts, ballet and baseball, and was an expert critic and writer about both. Like Markova, she had received the prestigious "Dance Magazine" award for outstanding contributions to ballet. She joined Markova at the Cincinnati College of Music. Markova taught dance with an emphasis on uninhibited and flirtatious performance. Manchester taught the history of ballet. Bill gave her students deep insights into the place of their craft in international cultural life. She also made sure that they and the wider community were well aware of the important star in their midst.

Modesty was not among Alicia Markova's virtues. She made her mark on Cincinnati. She was *Dame* Alicia, dignified in public. With Bill's direction we all knew that she was *Prima Ballerina Assoluta*. I remember one spring afternoon driving her and Bill Manchester back to our home for afternoon tea to comfort the expats. The conversation, unsurprisingly, was about ballet.

Rudolf Nureyev had recently visited to star in the season's opening performance. Shortly past his prime, his leaps had lost their breathtaking altitude but his dancing skills were nevertheless extraordinary (though whether that could be applied to his social skills is another story). I asked Dame Alicia what she thought about Nureyev. The corners of her mouth twitched and turned into that funny little grin. "Well," she replied, "the trouble with Rudy is that he burns the candle at three ends!"

As we reached our house, we passed the grassy bank by the barn. It was covered in a cloud of daffodils. As we pulled up at the house Dame Alicia asked, "Do you have a camera?" Moments later I found myself back beside the barn being directed to take photographs of her in a variety of artistic and graceful poses among the daffodils.

After tea we persuaded our guests to stay on for sherry. The talk turned to wine. Markova told a story about a group of men she met in New York. They were knowledgeable wine collectors, competitive rivals in their expertise and discernment. Every month they would meet at one of their homes and each would bring a bottle wrapped to cover the label and then compete to recognize its provenance. That particular month they ganged up to challenge their host whose arrogance as a wine snob irked them.

He took the proffered bottle and poured himself a sample. He swirled the golden liquid in his glass, "Obviously it's a robust white wine," he pronounced. He held it up to the light, "Product of a rare European terroir, from a southern slope I would venture." He raised the glass to his nostrils and sniffed delicately, "Distinctive bouquet." He raised the glass again and sipped. "Recent vintage, a nouveau . . . h'mm." He looked at each of them in turn. "I say, you chaps, you can't fool me."

That mischievous little twitch came to the corners of Markova's mouth and I fancied that I was glimpsing the girlish Alice Marks.

"No, you chaps, you certainly cannot fool me. I know what this is. This is piss." He paused and looked at each again. "The question is, whose?"

Piece of Cake

After several aborted attempts I finally retired and had enough time to pursue my lifelong avocation: writing. Efforts over the years included historical essays at school and university; news reports and editorials for our family newspaper and BBC radio; documents, reports, summaries and analyses for business; letters to friends and relatives; and stories, plays, verses, and limericks for entertainment.

Practicing my craft to serve a variety of audiences, I learned from all of these experiences. Stuart Wyton, BBC news editor, was a high impact mentor of a punchy, to the point, style. "Cut out the bloody adjectives, Richard," he muttered. "Cut out the bloody adverbs. Make the bloody verbs do the bloody work."

Once retired, I joined the Monday Morning Writers Group in Cincinnati to improve my skill through practice and constructive criticism. This led to an ambition to create a lengthy novel or history.

The first effort was *The Queen of Geometrica*, primarily for children curious about mathematics. The idea was sparked one day in Vermont by a cartoon drawing by my wife Penny, of a regal young woman and her servant with a triangular head. I dashed off the first chapter that afternoon, opening with the words, "What," said the queen, "shall I do today?" It went on to describe a cast of imaginary characters that dwelt in a land fascinated by mathematics whose ruling class spoke in Royalese when they did not know what to say nor wished to allow the common people to know what they meant.

I finished at least one chapter every Sunday and read it next day to the Monday Morning Writers Group, using their feedback to improve it. In less than two years I had finished a novel of thirty-three chapters, ending with, "This is the end, because thirty-three is divisible by three and eleven, both of which are prime numbers." Made it all up, no research, no fact checking, no concerns about critics who might point out errors or problems of plot or character.

The turning point came when my friend Ethan Stanley asked me to give a talk on my native Cornwall for his series on the history and culture of Britain for the Lifelong Learning Institute at the University of Cincinnati. I enquired whether twelve or only six three-hour lectures would be preferred. He firmly specified one sixty-minute lecture including fifteen minutes Q&A. I could do that off the top of my head given lore I had absorbed from my family throughout my childhood. I was steeped in Cornwall. Piece of cake.

My family were writers and historians. My brother-in-law Dr. Jack Ravensdale wrote the volume on Cornwall for the British National Trust history of Britain series. Much of his research was found among the dusty files of The Cornish Times, our family's newspaper of which my father was the editor, about the emigration of the Cornish tin miners to America during the depression of the 1870s. Jack and my sister Pam took me on field trips. My sisters assembled our family tree. My father being president of the Old Cornwall Society, my parents took me on outings to historic houses, castles and ancient monuments. I remember from his library The History of the Borough of Liskeard, published by his firm in 1856, the type hand set. As a boy I learned the compositor's trade with that very font. Today, the book is available on the Internet.

There were but a couple of details I was curious about for my talk, so I dug into my history books from Oxford. That is like thinking there is no harm in picking up a puppy just to hold it. You take it home with you. I could not tear myself away. Not since university had I enjoyed the luxury of exploring interlocking labyrinths of history. I ran amok. I was late for meals. I spent hours researching details, finding one clue that led to another, putting the story of one fascinating character into the context of national events and unexpectedly linking to another character, digressing from my proposed theme into alluring byways. Days of reading garnered enough material to necessitate proper organizing and even culling and inexorably to weeks of practicing my PowerPoint skills while painstakingly putting together a slide supported lecture, complete with an audio insert of "Trelawny", the Cornish national anthem.

We used to say in my BBC radio days that it took one hour of work to produce one minute of news. That is a lean estimate of what it took to dash that lecture "off the top of my head." Was it worth it? Evidently an engaged audience thought so. What a joy! Given the effort expended, it seemed a pity not to put all of that work to further use.

My wife Penny suggested I expand a little on my research and dash off a history of my native Cornwall. Given the scarcity of appropriate sources in Kentucky, this would certainly give rise to critical challenges to my scholarship. Not a pleasant prospect. So I settled on historical fiction; what answers research failed to dig up, imagination would supply. Piece of cake, but wisely I budgeted two years for the project.

Cornwall offers so much potential for plot themes. Inventors, explorers, adventurers, reformers and smugglers flourished. Richard Trevithick invented the high-pressure steam locomotive and the beam engine. Isambard Kingdom Brunel was the chief engineer of the Great Western Railway. Cornish miners and engineers emigrated all over the world. The Wesleys preached reform of the Church of England throughout the county. The Foot family preached Liberalism and teetotalism. The education of workers and the improvement of their conditions shook the rigid class system. Conflict progressively dented hierarchy as new ways of amassing and sharing wealth emerged. The choices had grown exponentially.

Simply deciding on the period, the topics, and the historical characters and events to create an authentic framework was next. While about it, why not write a trilogy? I could start with the Civil War, followed by my favorite period the eighteenth century, finishing with a flourish in the nineteenth and twentieth centuries with the contributions of the Cornish to America. I settled on a title, *The Cornish Chronicle*, sure to attract a publisher and a nice tie-in to my newspaper background.

To get started I would polish off Volume II. I would read up on the national background to develop a shape for the story that would be historically authentic. My tutor at Oxford, Stephen Watson, instilled in me his fascination with British history in the eighteenth century. His long awaited *The Reign of George III* was published. Watson had introduced us to Sir Lewis Namier's brilliant study of *The Structure of Politics in the Reign of George III*, about the maneuverings and influence peddling of the Duke of Newcastle, the Karl Rove of his day. Then I discovered a chapter devoted to Cornwall's extraordinary forty-four Members of Parliament and the "pocket boroughs" owned by wealthy landowners.

Being methodical, I wrote a plan and decided on a title that was sure to attract a publisher, *The Miner & the Viscount.* My outline reads: "The novel traces the lives of three main families from lower, middle and upper class backgrounds, the interrelationships of them and their offspring, the effects of them on the countryside, small towns in which they were raised, and the economic developments and changes that affected their lives. Fortunes of the aristocrats declined while those of the artisans rose as foreign competition decimated the tin and copper deep-mining industries. The rise of the Liberal Party and of the Methodist Church disrupted the old order established by the Tory Party and the Church of England."

Alas, connections kept popping up. I followed Winston Graham's popular BBC television series based on his eleven *Poldark* novels set in eighteenth century Cornwall, looking for suggestions about social history and manners and the Cornish dialect. Slow going.

However, Graham's acknowledgements include two men I remember. One was F. L. Harris, the Warden of the Workers Educational Association in Cornwall. Fred founded the Cornish Global Migration Programme and also recruited my sister and brother-in-law, Pam and Jack Ravensdale, as lecturers at the W.E.A. and encouraged their lifelong interest in adult education and local history. One of his classes taught me that there was a lot to learn about being an historian.

The other was T. S. Attlee, brother of Clement Attlee the Prime Minister. The evening they came to our home for dinner, my teetotaler father hospitably offered him a drink, hoping that his request might be met by the meager selection of 'medicinal' beverages whose dusty bottles graced our sideboard cupboard. Mr. Attlee asked for whisky, and fortunately our stock included a twenty-year-old Scotch and a soda siphon. The Scotch had been virtually untouched for the nineteen years my father had owned it, but the layer of dust gave the bottle a certain cachet. Our guest accepted the whisky but declined the soda. He then produced a silver flask from his waistcoat pocket, pronouncing, "I always bring my own water from a Scottish mountain burn. Many a host has a decent whisky, which good Scotsmen spent years perfecting. It's a desecration to spoil it with anything but the purest native water."

Taking him to heart I have drunk Scotch with pure water ever since.

To develop detail for my aristocratic characters, I mined the history and connections of three Cornish families: Eliot, Pitt and Robartes. Edward Eliot of the great Port Eliot estate in St. Germans, owned seats in the House of Commons including two for the borough of Liskeard and its thirty-two voters.

Thomas Pitt, the son of a poor rector, made his fortune in India. He traded with an Indian merchant for a great diamond that he sold for the French crown, and with the proceeds he bought ten country estates in England, including Boconnoc in Cornwall. His grandson was William Pitt the Elder who sat for his family's borough of Old Sarum and became one of England's greatest prime ministers and Earl of Chatham. His great grandson was the brilliant William Pitt the Younger who became prime minister at the age of twenty-four.

My villain was based on the Robartes family who had prospered as merchants and bankers and in the tin and wool trades and bought the great Lanhydrock estate. Richard also purchased a barony for ten thousand pounds, and the family later acceded to the higher title of Viscount Clifden. The last viscount died in 1974. My uncle Joseph Clemo was his steward. Viscount Clifden sat in the House of Lords as a Liberal, and I remember being introduced to him when he chaired a meeting in Liskeard at which I spoke when I was active in politics and president of the Oxford University Liberal Club.

The family of my miner was based on a W.E.A. pupil of Jack Ravensdale who worked in a slate quarry in Delabole where Jack spotted his intellect and drive and taught him economic history. Denis won a place at Balliol and read Politics, Philosophy and Economics. We saw something of each other at Oxford, although his politics were to the left of mine.

Oxford provided many an opportunity to enjoy one's fascination with history. At a dinner of the Queen's Historical Society our guest was historian and litterateur A.L. Rowse, fellow of All Souls', a specialist in the Tudor period, an authority on Shakespeare, and a passionate admirer of Queen Elizabeth. I particularly wanted to make a good impression since he was a fellow Cornishman, son of a St. Austell china clay worker who won a scholarship to Oxford. As one of my sources for the book I reread his *The Cornish in America*.

At these events one must ask intelligent questions, and I was prepared. After Rouse read his paper and the port had circulated the elegant senior Common Room, the questions began. Soon I judged my moment had come. I asked Dr. Rowse his view of the hypothesis of Professor A. Dixon Wright that the real reason for Queen Elizabeth so determinedly remaining the Virgin Queen is that she was in fact a hermaphrodite, a stray theory I had picked up during my browsings among the antique collections of the college library. What my hoped-for mentor said in reply I do not remember, but I do remember he was not very coherent and went purple in the face.

Later, James Adams the secretary wrote in his minutes, "The evening concluded when Mr. Hoskin asked a memorable pathological question."

But I digress. As I continued with my research I made fuller use of contemporary resources on the Internet. Google is a veritable collection of libraries on your lap. I found *The History of Liskeard* in the library of Harvard, a trove of information and stories of the local history, the details that enrich and enliven the dry accounts of events transpiring at the national level. I purchased a copy of this and many other rare and out-of-print treasures from Amazon. Google is a wonderful place to start and a signpost to multiple sources, but one has to be critically aware of apparent contradictions and inaccuracies. Much delight came from reading separate articles about different characters and perceiving commonalities and connections, weaving separate threads into a rich tapestry of story.

After more than a year, I was ready to start writing my book. As a caution, I read articles on how to write an historical novel, how to weave fiction into history, and how to avoid the perils of losing one's reader through concentrated dumping of the fruits of one's research so fascinating to the author. Advice on developing a complete outline was plentiful, but try as I might I could not imagine the future of my story beyond the broadest of sketches. I did describe my characters, including the fictional ones: their appearances, pedigrees, relationships, ambitions, conflicts, fears and failures. I strove to avoid my villain having distinctive grey eyes in Chapter 5 that had morphed to a piercing black by Chapter 17.

At last ready, I wrote a first chapter. Summarizing the importance of the history of my birthplace, Liskeard, I described a scene in the majestic Cornish landscape. I introduced the three aristocratic families, one of their stately homes, and the main mining characters, adding a gripping conflict. I read my chapter with pride to my writers group. I observed the reaction of the listeners and invented an evaluation method to gauge the reaction of my audience, ERBITS (Eyeballs Rolling Back In The Skull). Their feedback was courteous, somewhat encouraging, but summed up in a phrase as, "A bit overwhelming."

I broke that first chapter into three chapters and then got stuck. My frustration came out of the mouth of one of the characters who questioned, "I wonder what will happen next?" Then a miracle occurred and the characters took over. From then on the story flowed more or less fluently. Chapter after chapter was ready for a Monday read to an increasingly interested audience. After some two years Chapter 80 brought the story to a satisfying end, I proofread to eliminate typographical errors and I had a final manuscript. Next step, publication!

Then Penny kindly offered to edit the manuscript. It hardly seemed necessary, but I thought I might as well humor the old girl and invited her to go ahead. That led to six entire rewrites, front to back. What improvements came from the eye of a discerning reader and the mouth of a practiced writer! The most valuable contribution was the enrichment of the characters and the action by describing body language.

In the first draft I wrote, *William Pitt's gout was horribly painful.* After rewrite six, the scene read: *"Have the butler decant us your best port and bring me a footstool",* ordered Pitt. (The footman) *placed a stool to support Pitt's foot, which was as ever painfully swollen with gout . . . Pitt shifted his leg on the stool to ease the excruciating pain in his foot and reached for his glass.*

Piece of Cake ~ ~ page 168

In the fall of 2012 we set off for Cornwall with a virtual final manuscript to check a few details for authenticity and absorb the atmosphere and mystique of that land to perfect my descriptions of its beauty. We arranged to meet the people and visit the places that could provide the final polish. Peregrine Eliot, the Earl of St. Germans, showed us over Port Eliot. He told us how their neighbors paid for "honours" (titles) with money, relating how the Eliots were awarded theirs for influence.

The curator at the mining museum explained that the Geevor mine did NOT have ladders as I had described. His father had worked the Levant mine in one of the levels under the Atlantic Ocean, frightened when he heard the boulders rolling on the ocean bed above during a storm. We watched a Trevithick steam engine in operation. The Grand Bard of Cornwall, Maureen Fuller, provided Cornish language translations for passionate speeches by the miners. She suggested avoiding charges of inauthenticity by creating a fictitious mine named "Wheal Hycca", Cornish for "Mine Richard".

At Boconnoc, the seat of the Pitts, we were shown the house, told colorful stories, and entertained to lunch by the charming Fortescues whose family had inherited the estate in the nineteenth century. They had devoted their marriage to restoring the house, and we were their first guests for lunch. It was a warm and hospitable affair. Elizabeth Fortescue covered an eighteenth century mahogany library table with a plastic cloth, added a bottle of ketchup and a bottle of wine, and served traditional pasties from the local bakery.

Coming home with material made the final manuscript within reach, more interesting and rich in authenticity than ever. Penny had performed sterling service. Then a kind member of our writers group offered to help with what she described as "a little final burnishing" and also recommended substantial cutting. Maureen "Mo" Conlan was an experienced feature editor and book reviewer so I gratefully accepted. Three more front to back rewrites and burnishing to the tune of 25,000 *additional* words and we had . . . a "final manuscript".

Penny did the internal formatting and cover design. Were we done? She urged one more proofing, and I found a hundred and seventeen typos. I picked out a dramatic photograph of a Neolithic monument in Cornwall for the cover and proudly displayed it to the writers group. ERBITS! "You can't use that!" they protested. "It's a fertility symbol." A desperate call to my psychic and Cornwallophile daughter Sarah for the solution. "Ask St. Michael," she said, "he is the patron saint of Cornwall." Huh!

Mo Conlan called. "There is an amazing photo on the website by some guy called Michael, it's a place in Cornwall and it would make a great cover." It was and Penny worked it in: St. Michael's Mount.

The Miner & the Viscount was printed and published. I felt triumphant. Have I achieved fame and fortune as a world-famous author? Not yet, but it has been the most incredibly joyful experience and has produced friendships, contacts, memories and coincidences, adding up to the richest psychic income of my life.

Nearing Journey's End

On the occasion of my recent big birthday my children surprised me by joining the celebration here in Kentucky from their far-flung homes in Colorado and Pennsylvania. (Actually, they are getting a bit old to be described as children. Maybe "direct descendants" would better suit.) We all had a wonderful time. Over the next few days we talked and talked, and among other things I told them that I was close to completing these memoirs.

We wondered what might happen next. This led to concocting a plan: they would join me in traveling to Cornwall and exploring their ancestral heritage. Sharing my memories with them over the years had built a reservoir of interest that they were now eager to pursue while opportunity still exists. I was delighted. Together we would explore my birthplace, my childhood haunts, places my family lived, played, studied, worked: their heritage.

The Hoskin Cornish Heritage Tour was a great success. We characterized it with H words: heritage, happy, hoppy, historic, harmonious, heroic, humorous, heartwarming, hilarious, huperfragilisticexpialidocious, and Hoskinesque. We stayed in a cottage converted from a dairy barn on the farm where I spent summers as a boy. We went into Liskeard, the town where I was born and raised and we saw the window of my bedroom. We went up onto the moors and the village where my maternal grandparents grew up; then on to Looe and Polperro, the picturesque fishing ports where I caught mackerel from the quay side; and the expansive beach at Polzeath where our family had a summer cottage and I was christened.

Our route followed the path of my Cornish historical novel *The Miner & the Viscount,* climbing to the top of St. Michael's Mount, tunneling down the tin mine that inspired Wheal Hykka, stopping at the Trewellard Arms, and having tea at gracious Boconnoc House in the room where the banqueting scene took place.

The Royal Cornwall Show was a spectacular display of pedigree cows, sheep, pigs and goats, horse jumping, farm machinery, foods of infinite variety and prize-winning hard ciders. We walked through the nearby hamlet where my father and his sister rode their bicycles every Saturday to collect tuppence a week rent from the quarrymen living there in those days.

And we did research for my next historical novel, exploring the fascinating Wheal Martyn china clay museum, watching the workings at a great china clay pit, and visiting the hometown of the Quaker inventor of British porcelain, William Cookworthy.

There was so much we still wanted to do when other wishes pressed on our precious time together. By moving from Britain to America (a temporary move that became permanent) their mother and I deprived our children of living among their relatives and especially their cousins, on their mother's side as well as mine. So we made a point of staying with several of them to make up for lost time. For me, catching up with my former brother-in-law and his family proved an unexpected pleasure.

We crowned our Cornish Heritage Tour with a pilgrimage to the rambling old house in Kent where my big sister, dear Pat, now 95 years old, stubbornly lives alone. Her daughter Karen forewarned me with, "She's not as sharp as she was, and her sight has got worse, barely sees any more." Huh! When her son-in-law Tony passed the cakes at teatime and dropped a piece of shortcake on the carpet, Pat did not miss a beat. "That one's for the guests!" she pronounced.

My wife Penny had provided me with a final manuscript (seductive term!) of my new *Memoirs While Memory Lasts,* the printing of which had been delayed by the publishers. Pat's interest was whetted when I read her a couple of stories from our childhood. After the initial proofs were ready the first person in England to receive a copy hot off the press was Pat.

Pat's sight had deteriorated since she read *The Miner & the Viscount* with one eye and a magnifying glass, so Karen read more stories to her from *Memoirs While Memory Lasts* during her regular weekly visit and anticipated this would become a routine. The next time, however, Karen saw the book beside her mother's chair, along with her spectacles that she habitually resisted wearing. We talked across the Atlantic on Skype.

"I appreciated Karen reading to me," said Pat, "but when I read for myself I could imagine you in the room with me, telling me your stories. And I remembered what was going to happen next!" She glowed, and went on, "I've had to put them aside for a few days because I'm watching Wimbledon on television."

What joy. My stories engaged a bored old lady and stimulated her will to bring back, at least to an extent, her ability to see. Hers is absolutely the best reader review I have ever had. I am grateful to have made the effort to write these memories down and share them. Already I have added this story; perhaps soon I will have a finished manuscript.

Meanwhile, Karen is pursuing an idea that promises that *Memoirs While Memory Lasts* will bring more pleasure, at the other end of life's scale. When they were married in 1996 Karen and Tony went to the Gambia in West Africa. Their honeymoon gave birth to love for an entire community. Under a banyan tree in the village of Farato they observed a group of small children chanting the alphabet with their teacher. They decided to do something to help, not realizing their journey would take off as it did, and together began an amazing life of service.

Karen is a music teacher. Once home, she enrolled her children's recorder band in giving concerts in their village of Yalding in Kent. She raised enough money to buy a second-hand bicycle and persuaded an airline to fly it to Gambia free. Now the teacher could teach at two schools. They raised funds to provide school supplies, books, paper, and pencils. As the word of their work spread the donations grew and their support became more ambitious.

They started going to Gambia twice every year to support the village school, Karen training teachers, Tony overseeing projects and handing out money when he is satisfied with quality completion. A little house was built where they stayed during their visits. Back home they set up a British registered charity.

In 2006 they built two classrooms for 3-6 year olds and added two more a few years later. In 2016 they installed solar panels on the roof to supply electricity for the entire school. Now the classrooms are lit to enable students from the village to come freely to the school to study in the evenings. Then they dug a well powered by the solar energy that provides water for the whole community. They established a vegetable garden and built a wall to protect it from marauding animals.

They have built a computer suite to accommodate 15 pupils. One of the teachers has trained to a very high level to teach pupils from Grade 5-9. The computers are donated by people in England and pupils learn to take them apart and reassemble them so that the life of a computer lasts a lot longer than in UK where obsolescence rules. What is "old" to western schools and offices is very usable to their school. Most Gambian schools do not have computers available for the teachers let alone for the pupils the school provides a precious opportunity for very poor children.

Today, Farato boasts a school with 10 classrooms, elementary, middle and high schools, with 575 pupils aged 3 to 16, all wearing school uniforms, all being taught with progressive modern methods, and now being observed by the Gambian government as a flagship school to learn from their success.

They need help, especially with fund raising. With growth their needs have grown. I will give 100 free copies of my new book *Memories While Memory Lasts* to anyone who makes a donation to the Farato Gambia School, in whatever amount you choose. Perhaps this effort will take off and in future a portion of the proceeds will be applied to cover printing and shipping.

My Monday Morning Writers Group (that meets weekly in the Joseph-Beth bookstore in Cincinnati, Ohio) has taken this idea and run with it. First the members generously donated to launch the program. Then Karen said they would love to give books to senior pupils and staff to get them to write their own stories, to stimulate their own creative writing: a far cry from chanting the alphabet under the banyan tree. So these generous writers offered to "adopt" pupils, communicate over the Internet and help them with their writing, giving them feedback.

How wonderful. This idea is going to take off! Children in Africa will expand their education and the writing skills essential to leading fulfilling lives and contributing to their communities with the support and encouragement of writers around the world.

Will the stories ever end? Our trip has yielded enough interesting experiences and discoveries to stimulate another collection of memoirs, and the challenge of writing it will help to ensure that my memory lasts.

Eulogy

This collection of memoirs began with remembrances of my childhood long ago. It ends with the recent death of my oldest and closest friend in America.

The light that was Ken Schonberg burst into my life in 1971 when he brought his wife Joan and their three children from Scarsdale to Cincinnati in pursuit of a new career.

We met the Schonbergs at the house of English friends of ours and neighbors of theirs on Crabtree Lane in Indian Hill. I learned Ken had been born in Argentina, had lived in England and that they both enjoyed music. When obstacles present themselves, Schonbergs deploy creativity. Joan had trouble spelling the name of her new home, so she wrote a song and performed it that evening with guitar accompaniment. The chorus went, "C I N, C I N, NA, one T I."

I also learned that Ken's birthday was November 12th; he was born exactly one year later than my sister so I always remembered his birthday. This gave rise to my custom of celebrating his birthday with a limerick recording an event or achievement or adventure in Ken's life. For example:

> *A macho old gaucho from Rio*
> *Fathered of children a trio,*
> *With each decade of age,*
> *He turns a new page*
> *And lives life allegretto con brio.*

The next thing I learned was that the essence of Ken was zest, indeed enthusiasm. "Enthusiasm," a special word, means, "the god within us", and Ken fast became one of my favorite people.

It helped that he was an Anglophile. Ken fled his native Argentina and the dictator Peron for Britain in 1944 and replaced conscription and the goose-step in Peron's German-trained cadet force with volunteering to join His Majesty's army. Ken was officer material and was picked to attend the Royal Military College,

Sandhurst. He was commissioned in the cavalry, the 15th/19th The King's Royal Hussars, today a tank regiment.

The birthday celebration of Ken's heroic defense of the British Empire went as follows:

> *In his youth in defense of Great Britain*
> *Ken mastered the fine skill of sittin'*
> *On the seat of a horse —*
> *'Twas iron, of course,*
> *For Hussars that's really quite fittin'.*

Ken's experience with command led to his organizing happenings. He and Joan enlisted their neighbors in bringing to Crabtree Lane and its environs the first-ever and most fun community July 4th party they had ever joined in, complete with decorations, barbecues, drinks, inventive sports and contests never seen before.

Ken followed this up a year or so later by entering his Precision Lawnmower Marching Band Drill Team in the big Indian Hill July 4th parade, a hilarious contrast to the customary dignified horses and vintage cars.

On Christmas Eves Ken sparked a gathering around the crib set up by the village opposite the ranger station complete with live sheep and a donkey. He handed out candles and hymn sheets, recruited a brass ensemble from the high school band and conducted the caroling of old favorites, always culminating with *Silent Night*.

Then our families repaired to Crabtree Lane for feasting and playing the dictionary game and charades, memorably with David testing my knowledge of astronomy by challenging me to act out Uranus.

A later birthday celebration recalled the evenings like this:

> *For Ken, Christmas Eve in the village*
> *Started out with considerable spillage;*
> *It continued with games*
> *Of dubious aims,*
> *Thence to candlelit carols 'round the cribbage.*

And then there were the wonderful years at the Indian Hill Church, singing in the choir conducted by Tibby Plyler, who is with us here today, and performing in the summer outdoor musicals. Ken was type cast by Jackie Knapp to star in *Music Man*, inspiring the townsfolk of River City to make music and create entertainment. Then he got us to the church on time, rambunctiously playing Alfred Doolittle in *My Fair Lady*.

At lunch just before Christmas recently, Ken and I reminisced about our choir's mission to England in 1983. He sent me his journal of that inspiring trip when we stayed in the homes of hospitable parishioners of villages near Oxford and Cambridge and sang in college chapels and village halls and memorably in Ely Cathedral.

Here is his joyful account of punting in Cambridge when Ken took the pole position with an enthusiasm that varied inversely with his experience:

"We rented a punt, climbed in with our wine jug, and started down the Cam through the college lawns. Richard, our expert punter, started out in fine style, guiding us through the chaotic traffic of punts and canoes and many languages. The sun came out and gave a festive air to the scene, with its crowds of happy picnickers. Hazards like low trees and bridges made it even more fun, as Ken found out when he decided to take over the pole. Punting is not easy until you develop the knack.

"Banging off walls and other boats we made progress in a way, while the wine in the jug flowed freely. Ken found himself entangled in an overhanging willow and created a myth for himself by cussing the "damn weeds" as he tried to extricate the punt. Other members of the choir were observed on bridges laughing at us. Finally Richard took over again and got us safely back to the boatyard, all a little the worse for wear with an empty wine jug."

Enthusiasm got Ken into scrapes and creativity or delegation got him out again. And he helped others get out of scrapes. When Rev. James Metzger was fired from the Indian Hill Church, Ken donated outplacement counseling services at Schonberg Associates and provided Jim with an office for his job search. Then Ken helped organize the charter flight to St. Louis for the parishioners who introduced Jim to his new parish.

Ken and I shared knowing the English vocabulary word "swanning". It's a word that has the virtue of being little understood except by the cognoscenti. It means wandering through the countryside exploring for enjoyable experiences.

Swanning was put to good use when Joan Schonberg lost her long struggle with cancer and left us. As Ken grieved, my wife Penny and I joined him on a variety of swans. We went to an exhibition of Chinese art in Columbus, including the terracotta army and intricate embroidery; we explored the Indiana countryside arriving at the Chateau Pomije's vineyard and restaurant and leaving with faces smeared with barbeque sauce; and we enjoyed a free stay at the restored Mafia grand hotel in French Lick, Indiana, with yet-to-be-renovated bedrooms adorned with clanking radiators and peeling paint, all thanks to a special promotion and little interest in buying a timeshare equipped with hot tubs in mirror lined bathrooms.

Our intention was to cheer Ken up, but in fact our experience of Ken's companionship and his irrepressible optimism is what lifted us up.

Then Ken and I swanned across middle America, breaking the monotony of Kansas to find the Eisenhower Memorial Library in Abilene, but somehow ending up in the Greyhound Racing Hall of Fame. It was impossible to be bored in Ken's company, and on the rare occasions we ran out of conversation he filled the time with listening to a CD of Harry Potter, interspersed with my being cheerfully force fed with conjugating the Spanish verb *hablar* in all of its tenses and active and passive voices. He was, after all, one of the first moderators of the Institute of Lifelong Learning, teaching conversation in his native Spanish.

The trip passed quickly. We stayed with my kids in Colorado and explored Boulder with them. We raced the monstrous coal trains in Wyoming for mile after mile, and watched with awe as excavating machines the size of churches loaded mountains of coal out of moon-sized pits into the maw of an American economy guzzling energy. We swanned through the badlands of the Dakotas, marveling at the toughness of the pioneers who settled them. We pressed on to civilization in Chicago, where we stayed in Bunny Keep and shared in the barbeque-laced hospitality of Ken's delightful sons and their families.

And then another idea struck Ken, another group to lead, another activity to organize, one that would have a profound effect upon his life. He invited several of his friends to Crabtree Lane for an evening of poetry reading. With characteristic charm he asked us each to bring a favorite poem to share. He envisioned creating a regular gathering and calling it the Dead Poets Society, after the then popular Robin Williams movie.

As the evening progressed, Ken became distracted. One couple had brought a guest, a woman with a bright mind and a lively personality. They introduced her as Deborah Schultz. The Dead Poets Society never came to pass, but Ken and Deborah's marriage did, and they were together for the rest of his life.

Another good thing came out of that evening, the creation of a group of fine, upstanding, distinguished and virtuous gentlemen, who have ever since met for lunch on the second Friday of every month. We dubbed it the Fraternal Order of Filanthropists, the FOF. (There are some unworthies who whisper that the real name is the Fat Old Farts, but what's in a name?) We used to tell jokes, but now we can't remember the punch lines, so we share friendship and conversation and get to enjoy each other's company and stimulation. We owe it all to our peerless founder, Kenneth Carlos Schonberg. Many of us are here to celebrate Ken's life, some from far away.

Ken delights in a once monthly lunch
With an aging but still randy bunch,
Who get off each chest
With varying zest
Jokes lacking last lines with a punch.

I do have one regret. Ken left us a day or two too soon. For many years he and I had celebrated the changing of the years by sharing a vegetarian lunch between Christmas and New Year's Eve. The menu was always the same: several olives served up-straight in a martini glass, bathed in an aromatic, juniper flavored clear liquid to enhance their healthy nutrition. And then we toasted the rest of our lives. This year we narrowly missed seizing the day to celebrate yet another year of friendship.

My first thought when I heard the news from Deborah of my friend Ken's death was that life would not be the same without him.

But that is only partly true. Much of life will be just the same for many of us, better even, thanks to his example: pursuing multiple interests, exploring new things, progressive in thought, being open to imagination, enjoying fellowship, participating in lively discussions, supporting worthy causes, keeping up with family and friends.

Ken has forever affected our own way of living life, striving to live life to the full, with humor, with friendship, always with a positive attitude, whatever befalls us.

Enthusiasm: God within us.

Also from THE CORNISH CHRONICLE

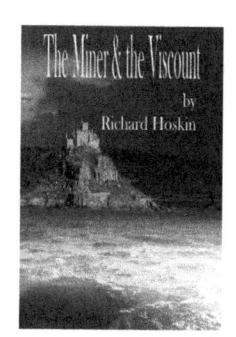

The Miner & the Viscount

by Richard Hoskin

Set in Cornwall in the turbulent C18th, when aristocrats and miners, politicians and preachers, struggled over power and the wealth that the great steam engines mined from the hard rock.

REVIEWS

UK — ... a masterful novel, rooted in history and industry, in social structure and humanity... style is lively, absorbing and consistent... an instinctive sense of balance... love and events entangle and shape each other, history and culture... lifelike as well as dramatic. — *Western Morning News*, Bert Biscoe

AUSTRALIA — The author cleverly weaves together stories of real and fictional families in a way that only someone with an intimate knowledge of Cornwall is able to do. Interest in Cornish heritage is undergoing a revival... no better starting point than Hoskin's carefully researched and entertaining book. — Dr. Jill Waterhouse

USA — ... a grand yarn. My pride in being Cornish swells at the stories of the historic worldwide leadership of my ruggedly independent people. — Cornish American Heritage Society, President

BUY www.amazon.com. See more reviews

VISIT www.theminerandtheviscount.com

Fall's Bright Flame

by Cynthia Osborne Hoskin

AMAZON READER REVIEWS

☆☆☆☆☆ Cynthia Osborne Hoskin, you are a skillful storyteller: you select the best details, just enough to pull your reader into your story. When the characters of a book seem so real that you think you could meet them in person any time and have a conversation with them, then you know you have read a good book.

☆☆☆☆☆ . . . grabbed me from the start so I knew it was my kind of novel: intellectually stimulating and a great "read" to boot. Along with her masterful dialogue and plot twists, I guarantee you will never know how this story turns out.

☆☆☆☆☆ A beautifully written story of a charming New England woman living and enjoying the many challenges and opportunities that life presents. The authors descriptions are vivid and the dialogue true. The language, tone and rhythm of this book knock me out.

BUY www.amazon.com. See more reviews
VISIT www.osbornehoskin.com